Beautiful

Chaos

grafohouse

Beautiful Chaos

© 2026 by Mary Jo Hansen

Published by Grafo House Publishing
in conjunction with Heart4Mexico
Tulsa, Oklahoma | Guadalajara, Mexico

ISBN
Hardback: 978-1-963127-55-3
Paperback: 978-1-963127-51-5
eBook: 978-1-963127-52-2

To contact the author or inquire about bulk discounts for churches and Bible study groups, visit h4mx.org.

Unless otherwise indicated, all Scripture quotations are taken from the New International Version ®, NIV® Copyright ©1973, 1978, 1984, 2011 by Biblica, Inc.® Used by permission. All rights reserved worldwide.

Printed in the United States of America
29 28 27 26   1 2 3 4

Lovingly dedicated to
my husband and best friend,
Dwight Hansen.
I'm so grateful to walk through life with you.

And in honor of the memory of
Erika Sierra Dahl
and Lina Esthela Solis Beltrán,
who poured so much of themselves into Nana's House
and are now rejoicing in heaven.

Contents

Introduction
Beautiful Chaos

The handcuffs were cold around my wrists. My daughter stood beside me, just as helpless. I couldn't believe this was happening.

The officer who shoved me into the truck leaned close and said, "Shut up, or I'll take you somewhere and drug you."

Not exactly the most comforting words I'd ever heard.

As we waited in the police station, a young girl was brought in and placed beside me. She looked lost—her eyes dazed. Phones rang. Time seemed to stop. I whispered the same prayer over and over: *God, please get us out of here.*

I knew that if they arrested you on a Friday, you stayed in a cell until Monday—and I couldn't let that happen. Especially knowing we had done nothing wrong. But if there's one thing I've learned through all my years in ministry and in chaos, it's that God has a way of showing up—sometimes to pull me out, and sometimes to teach me a lesson that will change everything.

That evening was one of the most dramatic—and probably traumatic—events in all the years we've been ministering in Mexico. I'll come back to the story later in the book because a lot happened leading up to that event that you need to know about. I will say this, though: That wasn't the first time chaos crashed into my life. And it certainly wouldn't be the last.

If you follow Jesus long enough, you notice something: His life was chaos, too. Crowds pressing in. Friends walking away. Storms rising out of nowhere. Authorities circling like wolves. From the outside, it appeared to be confusion, failure, and even defeat. Oh, how I can relate!

But here's the truth: Through it all, He was weaving redemption. A beauty you can't always recognize in the moment, but one you see clearly when you look back.

That's what this book is about.

It's about the nights I lay awake, wondering if the children in our care would ever truly heal. It's about the storms that broke me, the prayers that stitched me back together, and the miracles that still leave me in awe. It's about the good and the bad, the thrilling and the terrifying, the successes and the failures. But mostly, it's about God's perfect, redemptive grace.

As you read these pages, my hope is that you won't just see my chaos—you'll begin to recognize the beauty in your own. You'll see God's hand in the parts of your story that feel tangled, and you'll discover courage for the moments that threaten to break you. I want you to discover the God who steps into the mess, not to shame you or silence you, and not always to fix what feels uncertain or chaotic, but to steady your heart and surprise you with grace.

Chapter 1

Chaos Doesn't Get the Final Word

I grew up in a lot of chaos.

When I was six months old, back in 1961, a tragedy struck my family. It happened in Lewiston, Idaho, a quiet town where people still left their doors unlocked, trusting in the safety of their community.

But one night, something unimaginable happened.

A stranger slipped into my paternal grandparents' home. They weren't there at the time, and he likely hid in their bedroom closet, waiting in the shadows. My grandfather, unaware of the danger, walked into the room and came face to face with the man. The intruder had stolen a gun—one my grandfather had crafted with his own hands—and used it to murder both of my grandparents in cold blood.

The killer left the house, stole their car, and disappeared. To this day, we have no idea who killed them.

That event cast a dark shadow over my family. Fear took root—the kind that settles in and never quite leaves. I was just a baby when it happened, but the trauma shaped everything. My parents spoke of it matter-of-factly, as if it were just part of our story. Still, the fear lingered—unspoken and normalized.

When dysfunction becomes your baseline, you stop knowing what's "off." You learn to downplay pain. You lose your compass.

Many toxic things in my childhood were like that. Normalized. When dysfunction becomes your baseline, you stop knowing what's "off." You learn to downplay pain. You lose your compass. You struggle to recognize trauma in yourself—and even more, in others—because to you, it just feels like life.

My dad used to tell us stories about his parents. He kept their memory alive through laughter and affection. They became real to me through his words. But even as he spoke of them with love, I sensed the pain behind his eyes. He carried that grief silently for most of his life, only beginning to let it out in his late sixties.

On the outside, our home looked happy, and in many ways, it was. We lived in a beautiful suburban neighborhood in Campbell, California. My friends used to tell me we were "the happy family," which irritated me. Because part of it was real—we had genuinely good times—but they didn't see the chaos that was going on in our home.

We went to Mass every Sunday. My parents were involved in church, which was a big part of our lives. It brought many positives, along with some confusion. On one hand, my parents did some wonderful things that shaped my world in a very positive way. They marched with Cesar Chávez and the Latin community for better living spaces and pay. They took in some nieces and nephews who were getting into trouble and guided them onto a better path, and they helped several teens in our neighborhood.

On the other hand, their marriage was marked by tension and frequent, intense arguments. I loved my mother, but many of my childhood nightmares featured her trying to kill one of us. I'm sure those dreams came from the deep anxiety I felt. My mother wasn't affectionate, and I didn't understand that as a child.

The emotional climate in our home was often unstable. Although it wasn't always yelling, when they did yell, much of it happened in my parents' bedroom.

We were all affected by the legacy of trauma from my grandparents' murder, though no one said it out loud. My mother struggled with her emotions, which I didn't understand until later in life. It was only recently that some big secrets came out, and all of a sudden, the stress made more sense. Small things often became big explosions. She battled anxiety and eventually needed medication to manage it, but back then, many of those medications were addictive. That became a problem, too.

As a kid, I blamed my mom for everything. She was the one yelling, throwing things, and storming through the house. She was the one I feared. It wasn't until I was much older that I could look at her through a lens of compassion. I began to see the pain behind her rage. Still, her outbursts scared me. Her jealousy could spoil moments that should have been enjoyable.

My dad could be careless with his words, especially when it came to other women. Offhand comments cut deep into my mother's fragile self-worth. And then there was money—or rather, the lack of it. There was never enough. My parents lived above their means, and financial stress was a silent monster in our house. My dad spent years trying to earn my maternal grandfather's approval but refused to take his financial advice.

I felt that tension even as a child. Later in life, I'd come to recognize my deep fear around money as rooted in those early years.

My mother was eventually diagnosed with a rage disorder when I was in high school. But as a child and teenager, all I knew was that I never quite knew which mom I'd find when I walked through the door—warm and loving, or explosive and angry.

There were also things in our home that crossed major lines. My dad's sense of humor was wildly inappropriate. I developed early, and he'd make jokes about my body, saying I'd need bras made by "Omar the Tentmaker" or skis for shoes because my feet were so big. He would chase me around the house pretending to pull his pants down, and often he actually would pull them down, exposing his boxers while laughing hysterically. These weren't just awkward moments—they were personal violations. But I didn't have the words for it at the time.

It's challenging to explain dysfunction because it doesn't always manifest in an obvious manner. There were also beautiful and joyful moments in our family. I always knew I was welcome at home, even after I moved out. The love was there, but so was the drama. It never entirely stopped.

My safe place was the street we lived on—Central Park Drive, a picture-perfect suburban neighborhood. My friends were my refuge. That street was my world, full of laughter and adventure. It's where I found freedom and joy.

School, on the other hand, was harder. I struggled with dyslexia, was uncoordinated, and was never considered pretty by the boys. The fear I carried at home was subtle, but at school, it turned into shame. Rejection was loud there. Still, I have some good memories. Some teachers believed in me, and when I felt seen, I thrived. But if I sensed rejection, I retreated deep into self-hatred.

By high school, I was bulimic, depressed, and sometimes suicidal. I saw a psychologist, but healing didn't happen there. It happened in the high school choir. It happened with my girlfriends. It happened in the pockets of love that broke through the chaos.

At home, trauma had become the norm. That's the dangerous part: when chaos becomes familiar, you stop recognizing it for what it is. You learn to survive it. And survival becomes your story.

Until one day, you reject the story. You wake up and say: "This isn't love, and it isn't home. And it never should have been."

Here's the beauty: Chaos may have shaped me, but it doesn't get the final word.

When I was nineteen, I tried to give my heart to Jesus, but I didn't feel like I fit into church culture at all. At night, I sang in lounges with a young woman I'd met at my local Catholic church. She was incredibly talented, with a streak of wild-ness that drew people in. After we sang, some of my friends and I would drift to late-night parties, places thick with music and overflowing with alcohol. I drank far too much. I was often the girl chugging a fifth of Bacardi while everyone around me cheered.

Chaos may have shaped me, but it doesn't get the final word.

It was a reckless season, marked by few boundaries. When a friend asked me to care for his beautiful home while he and his wife traveled through Europe, I treated it like another party venue. I didn't take care of his things, or his space, or the trust he had given me.

I didn't use drugs, but alcohol was more than enough. On the outside, I looked bold and unbothered. On the inside, I was quietly unraveling, secretly battling an eating disorder no one could see.

The ground beneath me kept shifting. The guy I was crazy about confessed he was gay. One by one, my best friends began discovering the same truth about themselves. Everything I had assumed was stable started to fall apart.

And I was deeply, painfully miserable. I believed in Jesus and knew I needed Him. I just didn't know where I belonged with Him. I didn't know how to trust Him. I felt broken.

My parents saw me as a wreck; but in my eyes, they were unraveling too. They even asked me to buy marijuana for them once. I hated weed. I had tried it and had an awful experience.

Meanwhile, my two little sisters were still living at home. Things were getting worse.

While my parents were on a trip, I was at home when I got a phone call. One of my sisters had stolen something from a store. She was a young teen, with her friends, and did something dumb. On a scale of evil things to do, this was not the worst thing in the world. Still, the police were involved, which meant I had to tell my parents. Just thinking about the drama that would follow, especially involving my mom, made me sick with nerves.

When my parents came home, I pulled my dad aside and told him what had happened. I pleaded with him to wait until morning to tell my mom so we could all sleep peacefully that night. But late that night, while I was asleep, I woke to screaming. I jumped out of bed and saw my mom dragging my sister down the hall by her hair. The reaction was wildly over the top for the crime that had been committed. I was exhausted by the constant drama.

I have a strong voice, so I yelled, "STOP!" We locked eyes in a long stare, and she finally let go. There were many moments like this with my mom, until one day, when she became violent with another sister, I saw something different in her, a deep insecurity and fear. That time, I grabbed her arms and said, "Mom, we love you. Please calm down. Everything will be okay."

Another night, I came home to pure chaos. My mom and sisters were hiding upstairs. For the first time, I saw my dad drunk, stumbling outside in his boxers, slurring that he wanted to die. Inside, red lipstick scrawled obscene, derogatory words about my mother across the walls and mirrors. I never found out what fully happened that night, but it involved a party, another man, and something that shattered my dad.

Eventually, I couldn't take it anymore. I moved out. Later, when my parents relocated, I lived in a small basement apartment they owned. I kept my distance unless one of my sisters needed me.

I desperately wanted the chaos to calm down. During that season, God took my hand. Slowly I began to get glimpses of what peace felt like. I remember one incident in particular, after I turned twenty. I had walked across the street to a small park. I had my Bible with me, and I was sitting in the grass, crying out: "Jesus, I can't do this anymore. I need You, but I don't know how to follow You. Please speak to me."

I opened my Bible and landed on Isaiah 62:2–4.

"You will be called by a new name
      That the mouth of the Lord will bestow.
You will be a crown of splendor in the Lord's hand,
      A royal diadem in the hand of your God.
No longer will they call you Deserted,
      Or name your land Desolate.
But you will be called Hephzibah, [My delight is in her]
      And your land Beulah [Married];
For the Lord will take delight in you,
      And your land will be married."

Something broke open inside me. Those words reached every part of me that felt abandoned, broken, and unlovable. God was giving me a new name. I wasn't forsaken—I was His delight.

The next day, I attended church and gave my life to Jesus.

At first, I thought Christians were weird, and they thought I was strange. The way I dressed and spoke alarmed some people. But I stuck with it. I made friends. I joined the choir and got involved in music and drama, which were things I loved. I also started volunteering, giving Bible studies to girls in juvenile hall. I dreamed of opening a transition home for them—someplace safe, where they could find hope.

Real transformation is rarely instant. It unfolds slowly, not overnight.

I still had an eating disorder. I was still smoking. I was still deeply insecure. But I loved the Lord, and little by little, healing came.

People often say that giving your heart to Jesus transforms you. And it's true—but real transformation is rarely instant. It unfolds slowly, not overnight.

Unfortunately, in this new life I had found, I thought I had to be perfect. I put my past in a box and tried to live up to a standard no one could meet. I let go of lifelong friends—friends I should've kept, because I didn't think they fit my new "church life." I had partied, smoked, and drunk too much. Many of my friends were gay. In my immature thinking, I believed walking with Jesus meant walking away from them.

Now I know better. I was trying to be good. Trying to belong. But the beauty of grace is this: It finds you right where you are. In the healing. In the becoming. In the chaos.

Chaos was my first language, the rhythm I grew up in. But God, in His mercy, began teaching me how to turn that chaos into purpose.

Chapter 2

A Whisper of Peace

I had spent nearly a year faithfully attending church, searching for something more—something more profound. One Sunday, a missionary named Floyd McClung from Youth With A Mission (YWAM) came to speak. He shared stories from the red-light district of Amsterdam, where he and his wife were living among the most broken and forgotten people, offering them love, hope, and Jesus.

As he spoke, I felt my heart pounding so hard it almost drowned out his voice. I knew deep in my bones that this was what I was made for. "Here I am, Lord. Send me" (Isaiah 6:8) echoed in my spirit, even if I didn't know the verse by heart yet.

There was a YWAM base in Los Angeles, just six hours from my home in San Jose. I had some money coming to me soon and set my heart on doing a Discipleship Training School (DTS). But when I went to my pastors, they weren't in agreement. My parents weren't excited either. Still, I couldn't ignore what was stirring inside me. It wasn't a fleeting idea—it was a calling. "His word is in my heart like a fire, a fire shut up in my bones" (Jeremiah 20:9). That's how it felt. I had to go.

I called the school. A man with a voice like Bob Dylan answered. I asked if it was too late to join the DTS. I explained to him that I didn't have the money in hand, but that someone owed me enough money to cover the costs, and when it came in, I would pay the school. He simply said, "Get a plane ticket. We'll worry about the rest later." So, I did.

That step of faith marked the beginning of a new chapter. And though it might sound odd, the first time I ever truly felt peace in my life was sitting on the grass at the YWAM base, strumming my guitar. The noise of my life quieted. I had found my little oasis. I had found my people.

But peace is often followed by trials. Just when it came time to pay the school fees, all my money was gone. My dad had forged my name and taken the funds, promising to pay them back—but we both knew he couldn't. Shame hit hard. I felt like I had failed before I even started. But God was working even then. I had planned to go to Amsterdam, but instead, the handsome school director named Dwight Hansen asked me to stay and serve on staff. I said yes.

He was the guy who answered the phone with the Bob Dylan voice. God was rewriting my plan.

It was during that season that I became close friends with Dwight, as well as with Rod, who was in my Discipleship Training School and was an excellent musician. We played music together— Dwight and Rod played guitar, and all of us sang vocals. Dwight and I started spending a lot of time together. I liked

I felt like I had failed before I even started. But God was working even then.

him, but he made it clear we were "just friends." I was okay with that—until I wasn't.

I went home to San Jose for a short visit. When I returned, Dwight was waiting in the parking lot. He missed me. I could feel the shift.

A few weeks later, on a beach in Mazatlán during a six-week outreach trip, with a large team we were both leading, he asked me to be his girlfriend. But I told him, "I don't want a boyfriend. I want a forever relationship. I want to get married." Six weeks later, we were married.

Yes, it sounded unbelievable to everyone else. But to me, it felt like a sense of peace and purpose. It felt like God. My family showed up for the wedding, including my grandparents, my uncle, my siblings. It was a simple celebration on the YWAM base. No fancy dress, no grand reception. Just love and commitment before God and our people. All I ever wanted was to marry my best friend—and I did.

We served together for five years, leading schools, traveling with students, and pouring out what God had poured into us. I became the base cook despite having zero experience, and somehow, I loved it.

Dwight, noticing the subtle anxiety in me—the expectation of emotional chaos—asked me one day something I'll never forget: "Why are you always waiting for some crisis to happen?"

I had grown up with chaos, and it had become my "normal." But in this new life, I was learning a new kind of chaos: *beautiful* chaos. The kind that comes from living on the mission field. When we traveled to the villages in Mexico, we used tarps to create makeshift showers and improvised hoses for water. The water often shuts off. Rats would run up and down the drainpipes, completely freaking me out. We slept in tents on the ground. One time, Dwight fell very ill with typhoid, and a rat fell on his back while he was trying to sleep. Chasing rats out of drainpipes at midnight was not a pleasant task. There were conflicts with students or staff at times, but we navigated them with peace and grace. No screaming matches, no blowups. I began to realize that, for the first time in my life, those fruits were growing in me.

After a few years, we felt ready to start a family. But it didn't happen. Month after month, disappointment piled up. Tests and diagnoses confirmed it: infertility. That word landed like a brick on my heart.

All around me, other missionary couples were having babies. I felt broken. Less than. Inadequate. But Dwight? He wasn't shaken. He loved me as I was—never pressuring, never blaming. I was the one who carried the shame.

It was in that pain that I had to wrestle with my worth before God.

Our five years on the YWAM base were years of fire and refining, and somewhere in the mix of all that joy, loss, community, and calling, I discovered that even when life doesn't unfold the way we hope, God is still at work in the unfolding. Eventually, we began to feel a tug to leave YWAM.

We were invited by my former pastors to San Jose, California, to interview for a youth pastor position. At the time, we were already feeling a gentle nudge from the Lord that it was time to move on from the YWAM base, so we decided to explore the opportunity.

Not long after settling in, we got a phone call from Dwight's mom. His sister, Mary Kay, was pregnant and in a tough place. She was already raising twin boys with Fragile X Syndrome, along with a young daughter, entirely on her own. She asked if we would consider adopting her baby.

We talked to people who had adopted, and almost every single one said, "Don't adopt from a family member—it'll get too messy." But we took time to pray. We didn't want to make such a big decision out of emotion or guilt. Still, in our hearts, it felt right. We believed God was asking us to say yes.

Nothing about our circumstances said, "Ready for a baby." But something in us— and especially in me—knew this was the path.

From a practical standpoint, it didn't make any sense. We didn't have a permanent home. Our funds were low. Our car was an old truck with manual steering that gave me a workout every time I drove it. Nothing about our circumstances said, "Ready for a baby."

But something in us—and especially in me—knew this was the path.

Dwight was genuinely excited about the baby, but I began to notice a heaviness, an unspoken sadness, stirring beneath the surface. He wasn't himself. Around that time, some missionary friends came to visit. They filled our home with stories from the field—adventures, miracles, risks, and the raw beauty of living on the edge for Jesus. When they left, Dwight grew quiet.

Then, one day, he finally spoke words that broke my heart: "I feel like God fired me."

I knew he was serious. He wasn't just feeling left out; he was grieving a loss of purpose.

A few days later, we sat across from each other at a McDonald's, of all places. We were just two tired people eating fries and trying to figure out their lives.

I looked into his eyes and, without thinking, the words spilled out: "We're missionaries. Let's go to Mexico."

It was as if the room shifted. The noise faded. And in that one moment, peace wrapped around us like a blanket. We didn't need to analyze it—we just knew. God was not finished with us. He was redirecting us.

So, we said yes.

Yes to the baby.

Yes to stepping back into our calling.

Yes to returning to the mission field—this time to Mazatlán, Mexico, where Dwight's sister and brother-in-law were leading the YWAM base.

We made plans, but God was already miles ahead of us, paving the way. Just like Proverbs 16:9 says: "In their hearts humans plan their course, but the Lord establishes their steps."

Looking back, I can say with certainty that God's plan is always better than our own. But sometimes, walking through the doors He opens is a battle. Unknowns, challenges, and sacrifice cover the path. The life I imagined looks nothing like the life I live today—and yet, in so many ways, this is better. But getting here has required surrender. I had to let go of things I once held tightly to walk in the fullness of what He had for me.

We lived in Mazatlán for ten years. When we first arrived, we served with Youth With A Mission, but over time, God began to stir something different in our hearts. We felt called to stay, to go deeper, to become part of the community—not just visitors or volunteers, but a genuine part of the family. So, we stepped away from YWAM once again and joined a local church in Mazatlán.

There was so much to learn about the language, the people, the culture. We didn't want to live in a bubble. We wanted to immerse ourselves, to walk the dusty roads, eat at the little corner shops, celebrate the local festivals, and cry with those who mourned. We wanted real, lifelong friendships. And we dreamed of planting churches—places where people could encounter Jesus in their own heart language and cultural expression.

Around 1991, that dream began to take shape. We started planting churches in the mountains north of the city. The area was remote, rugged, and breathtaking—but it wasn't exactly safe. There were warnings, but we didn't always know what we were walking into. And maybe that was a blessing.

Sometimes, *not knowing* is what frees you to take giant steps of faith.

We were still stumbling through Spanish, still figuring out the subtle layers of Mexican culture, but we showed up with our hearts wide open. And that was enough. God met us in our weakness and used it all— our broken Spanish, our awkward missteps, our wide-eyed wonder.

Those years taught us that mission work isn't about having everything figured out. It's about being willing to go where God sends you and trusting He'll fill in the gaps.

Our baby, Jesiah, was growing fast, and we adored him. Our little family was filled with joy, laughter, and a sense of purpose. I loved being a mom—it felt like the most natural thing in the world. And as time went on, that deep, aching desire to grow our family began to rise again in my heart. I couldn't shake it.

One day, I brought it up to Dwight. I told him I wanted to adopt another baby.

He paused. I could see the question in his eyes. "Why can't we just be content with the family we have?" he asked gently. "We're not citizens here. We live in Mazatlán, Mexico. It's doubtful we'd even be allowed to adopt again."

I didn't want to argue. I understood Dwight's logic, but it felt like he was shutting the door on something sacred stirring inside me. Still, I listened—until he added one more thing.

"If you meet a pregnant woman who wants to give up her baby for adoption and asks you to adopt the baby, then maybe we'd consider it. But otherwise, forget about it. I don't want you getting your hopes up."

The words stung more than I would have expected.

Forget about it?

How do you forget about a desire that feels woven into your soul?

We argued. I felt shut down, pressured, and hopeless. And somewhere between the words and the silence, I began to pray—not just for a baby, but for God to make a way where there seemed to be none.

> *How do you forget about a desire that feels woven into your soul?*

One day, Dwight was preaching on an open-air platform just down the road from our house. A team from YWAM had come to Mazatlán to do street evangelism, and Dwight had agreed to share a message.

I was still a bit miffed—if I'm honest, I didn't feel like being the supportive missionary wife that day. My heart was still tender from our argument, and I had quietly decided to take Jesiah to the beach instead. The ocean was just a short walk away, and the idea of letting the waves wash over my frustration sounded far more appealing than sitting through another evangelistic event.

But as I got Jesiah ready to go, I felt it—that slight, undeniable nudge in my spirit: *Go to the meeting. Not the beach.*

I almost brushed it off. I had a hundred reasons to ignore it, but I couldn't shake the sense that I needed to be there—not for Dwight, not for the crowd, but for something I couldn't quite name.

So I shifted plans. I scooped up Jesiah, packed a few snacks, and made my way down to the platform, still carrying a bit of attitude but curious enough to obey that nudge.

I had no idea what awaited me, but it would change everything.

I met a young woman there who was part of the YWAM group in Mazatlán. In conversation, I learned she was from the same hometown as my parents, and that her uncle had led my father to the Lord years ago. That kind of divine connection always made me smile.

I figured she was the wife of one of the leaders. I mentioned to her that Jesiah was adopted and that I hoped to adopt another baby one day. She let me know she needed to do something.

Ten minutes later, she came back.

She was pregnant—I could see that clearly—but what she said left me floored. "I'm giving this baby up for adoption," she told me. "I come from a loving family, but I went through a hard time and ended up pregnant. I want this baby to have a father and a mother. And I would like you and your husband to adopt my baby."

I was stunned. Dwight's words echoed in my mind. She said exactly what he'd said—and here she was.

It was a big step of faith. We didn't have a home in the United States, since we were living in Mexico at the time, yet we had to complete the adoption there. Everything seemed to be working against us, and the process was nerve-wracking. But in 1991, we officially adopted our daughter, Rebecca Mary Hansen. I gave her the name "Rebecca" after her birth mother and "Mary" after my own, blending both parts of her story into one. Both of our children's adoptions were open, allowing connection and truth to be a part of their beginnings.

For years, I thought we'd live in Mazatlán forever. I loved it deeply. But once again, God had a different plan. The founding pastors of the church where we were serving began heading in a direction we didn't feel aligned with—not wrong, just not the same calling.

Leaving was hard. But it led us to Tepic, the capital city of the state of Nayarit, Mexico, where God would birth something new: La Fuente Church and, later, my life's passion—Nana's House.

In the chaos, the curveballs, the divine interruptions, I could always hear whispers of peace. They were all part of the story. Jesus' story.

Chapter 3

Choosing to Stay When Walking Away Feels Easier

We thought we were moving to Puerto Vallarta. That was the plan—or at least what we thought was the plan. But God had something else in mind, and we found ourselves landing in Tepic, Nayarit, Mexico.

Now, even some Mexican nationals I meet have never heard of the city we serve in. And my friends in Mazatlán were baffled. "Why Tepic?" they'd ask, their faces scrunched up in confused sympathy.

I didn't have a flashy answer, because the truth is, it isn't glamorous, and we didn't choose it for what it could offer us. We knew it was the right fit, and the more I looked, the more I found wonderful things about the region. Years before moving there, I had visited San Blas—just twenty-five minutes away—and fallen in love with the jungle and the beautiful mountains surrounding the area. Additionally, being within reach of Puerto Vallarta and Guadalajara was a significant benefit.

Our kids weren't thrilled to leave Mazatlán. They missed their routines and their friends, but they adjusted far better than I expected. Honestly, they made me proud. Change is never smooth, and we had our share of bumpy days, but we weathered it together. As they grew older and were doing well, I found myself with more room to lean into ministry. That was their gift to me. They weren't perfect, but I wasn't raising perfect. I was raising real. And real they certainly were.

What if we opened an orphanage? Not just an institution, but a home where children could truly belong?

Children in need have always captured my heart, and I began to dream out loud. *What if we opened an orphanage? Not just an institution, but a home where children could truly belong?*

At the time, we had one main supporting church behind us. We shared the vision, and they responded with enthusiasm. They even picked the name. We rented the house next door to our house and began preparing, believing they would back it financially because that was the promise they had given. That was the original idea. But somewhere along the way, the enthusiasm never turned into action. No formal announcement was made, no commitment given, no plan laid out—just silence. I think the idea of sending money each month was more difficult than they anticipated.

And suddenly, without warning, the whole thing fell into my lap.

I hadn't prepared to raise the funds. I wasn't ready to carry the weight, although I spoke Spanish and lived right next door to the house where the kids were staying, so it was obvious to me that I would be leading this ministry. But then came the twist: They insisted that the pastor's wife in the U.S. would be in charge—even though she didn't speak Spanish and didn't live in Mexico. It was a strange setup. Awkward. Uncomfortable. And yet, somehow, we kept moving forward.

In 2008, we opened the doors of Nana's House.

That same year, Mexico's president declared an all-out war on drugs and those who sold drugs. And just like that, our sleepy little town turned into a front line for the war that had begun. Nana's House was born right in the middle of chaos—not the beautiful kind, but the dangerous kind. Still, we were exactly where we were supposed to be.

Was it where I wanted to be? No, not even close. But God was with us, and looking back now, I'm still blown away by His grace.

From 2008 to 2011, Tepic, Mexico, endured one of its darkest chapters. Violence exploded. It wasn't distant news anymore; it was right outside our doors. Our city became a battlefield, and every day carried an edge of uncertainty. Sometimes it felt like the very air was poisoned with fear—thick, suffocating, impossible to escape. Even in moments of calm, you could feel it lurking, a heaviness pressing down, reminding you that danger was never far away.

One thing I learned quickly is that people who are far from violence glamorize things like drug cartels. It's almost like they think it's cool or edgy to know about gangs or be close to danger. But when you're living in it—when you're raising kids in it—it's a whole different story.

There's nothing glamorous about it. It's not exciting or thrilling. It's heartbreaking and frightening. It's the kind of awful that leaves you stunned, speechless, and unsure of what to say. I've seen things I'll probably never talk about because they're just too horrible to put into words.

Even in the middle of all that, we never really considered leaving. Not because we were fearless, but because we knew God had called us to this place. We trusted Him to protect us, and we believed that if He had placed us here, He would give us the strength to keep going.

Looking back, I realize how much He carried us during those years. We just kept putting one foot in front of the other, choosing to stay rooted in love and faith, no matter what was going on around us.

From the very beginning, I loved having Nana's House right next door. Our first little girl was Isabel. She was a sweet, calm little girl. Before long, we had a full house—ten beautiful girls, each carrying stories far heavier than any child should.

We had help from a young couple, Cynthia and Nile. Cynthia had the gentlest heart and a special way with the kids. They were a huge blessing in those early days. Eventually, they moved away to start a family of their own in Nile's hometown, where it was safer. I understood their decision. When Cynthia and Nile left, a young woman named Erika stepped in. She became the new house mom. Her mother, Lina, was the cook at first and later served as a house mom. Erika's sister, Sonia, was involved during that time as well, though not yet full-time.

These three remarkable women helped shape Nana's House. They were an essential part of what Nana's House is today, staying through both the hardest and the most beautiful seasons. Sonia is still serving at Nana's House as a key leader. Erika later married and moved to North Dakota. Sadly, she passed away suddenly at the age of forty-five.

Lina, lovingly called "Grandma," deeply loved Nana's House, and the girls loved her just as much. She battled cancer with courage, but she passed away in 2022.

Slowly, Nana's House began to grow, and more people stepped in as volunteers. We were all learning together how to function as a team and how to understand and respond to the deep brokenness carried by some of the children.

We had a few girls who would have screaming fits full of rage and pain. It wasn't just acting out, either. It was soul-level grief. They were wonderful kids, but they had been through so much. Abuse, loss, and abandonment were layered on top of each other. Oddly enough, my childhood with a mom full of rage had given me a strange kind of preparation. I knew what that kind of fury looked like. I had seen it up close. And because of that, I felt like I had a way to connect with the girls in their meltdowns. I wasn't scared of their storms. I could sit with them in them.

We needed a van to transport the girls to school and their various activities. Then, out of nowhere, we received a miracle donation that let us buy one. I decided to have it painted white with a touch of pink—just enough to make it sweet, not flashy.

Well, it turned out full-on Pepto-Bismol pink.

It honestly looks like a Barbie van. I think the whole town recognizes it by now. Subtle it is not.

When we first opened Nana's House, I made sure to go around to all the neighbors to tell them

I had a way to connect with the girls in their meltdowns. I wasn't scared of their storms. I could sit with them in them.

what we were doing: that we had opened an orphanage and were working directly with Child Protective Services. However, our neighbors weren't entirely convinced that we were rescuing girls, and before long, rumors began circulating. Some people even accused us of trafficking girls.

The police visited the house on multiple occasions. They showed up so many times that one day, I'd had it. They were scaring the girls and stirring up fear instead of helping. I marched over to Nana's House, looked straight in the eyes of a whole group of police officers with machine guns, and let them have it.

I told them, "Stop accusing us of things that aren't true! I won't take it anymore. We're here to stay. We're not going anywhere. Call CPS to confirm our identity." They backed away from me as I spoke. Considering all our town was going through, I still can't believe I did that, but it worked. They backed off.

The neighborhood where we started Nana's House is the same neighborhood I live in today. It was a strong place to begin, because once the community understood what we were doing, they became welcoming, helpful, and supportive. At the same time, people from our church stepped in in countless generous ways. Doctors cared for our sick children without charging. A dear family who runs a beautiful elementary school opened their doors and enrolled many of our children tuition-free. Others volunteered their time to give music and art lessons.

We were gaining trust here in Mexico, but we still needed financial support from the United States and Canada in order to keep going. I quickly learned that fundraising for a nonprofit is like walking around with a sign that says, "Please judge me." People want to know if you're worth investing in. They want proof you'll stick it out and not disappear when things get tough. You must survive the storm before you can earn respect or trust.

All I wanted to do was run the home. That part came naturally to me—caring for the kids, creating a safe space, keeping things running day to day. But that wasn't all God was calling me to. His plans stretched far beyond what I imagined, and they pulled me straight out of my comfort zone.

The legal battles, the endless fundraising, the meetings with CPS, the police, and government officials—none of that felt natural to me. Fundraising, especially, was the most intimidating of all. The thought of being that charismatic, spotlight-loving speaker who could captivate a crowd and raise vast sums of money? That was never me.

I'm still not that person. But God, in His way, did so many amazing things despite all my fears. He provided, not because I was confident or skilled, but because He is faithful.

Back then, even the pastors who supported us had never really seen me in a leadership role. I know they were skeptical. The truth is, I have one real talent: I'm a mom. I love working with kids, and I'm good at interacting with them. Loving the unlovely, the broken, the ones the world overlooks—that's what Jesus made for.

It's not glamorous. Not even close.

One time, a well-known preacher came to visit. He took one look around and said, "What you're doing here is like shoveling crap." I was stunned. I think he meant it as a compliment—like, gritty, humble work—but it didn't land that way. I was offended. Hurt, honestly. I wanted him to see the beauty, not just the mess.

However, the truth is that it is messy. Chaos, heartbreak, and trauma manifest in a hundred different ways. And still, I see beauty everywhere. These are kids. Real kids, with real stories. And all I can see is potential—so much potential it almost feels foolish.

The hope I carry for them is wild and stubborn. Maybe it's naïve. Perhaps it doesn't make sense. But I can't let go of it. I won't let go of it. I've had to learn a lot along the way—about love, about limits, about letting go. But if believing in a child too much is my biggest mistake, I'm willing to make it a thousand times over.

It's not just me believing the best for these children. It's also all the staff and volunteers, as well as my husband, who has always supported the craziness I have brought into our lives. I could never take all the credit for Nana's House's success. The reality is that it's God and His crazy love and fierce commitment to the brokenhearted, especially children who had no control over their circumstances.

I had many ideas about how Nana's House should be run. In retrospect, like most visionary ideas, my plans needed to be shaped and molded. For example, when I came to Mexico, I thought I would be fluent in Spanish within six months. That wasn't even close to reality! I am deeply thankful for my team and for God, who guided us and gave us the grace to let go of ideas that simply didn't fit.

Even when things don't turn out the way we imagined, they often become something deeper and more meaningful than we first hoped.

I think as we get older, we can look back and see that even when things don't turn out the way we imagined, they often become something deeper and more meaningful than we first hoped. Vision and ideas usually begin with an idealistic picture, but over time they are shaped, strengthened, and refined by real life, and in that process is often where the greatest beauty is found.

My heart was in the right place when I started Nana's House, but I had no idea how much I still had to learn. I wanted the best for these girls. I believed that if we, as a team, could just provide a stable and loving environment, everything would fall into place. That hearts would heal. That safety and consistency would somehow erase the pain.

But that's not how trauma works.

Trauma is messy, complicated, and stubborn. It refuses to follow our rules. It won't loosen its grip just because we love harder or mean well. Sometimes people never fully heal. That was a hard truth that I wasn't prepared to face.

Our original plan was simple: take in ten girls and give them a home. But the girls had brothers—little boys with nowhere to go and the same empty look in their eyes. So, we opened a house for boys.

We were growing fast but not surviving financially. I was living in trauma myself—trying to figure out how to raise funds while keeping the lights on and the kids fed. I didn't want to let the children down. I didn't want to let our staff down. I carried the burden of provision like a boulder strapped to my back. My biggest mistake? Believing that if I couldn't raise the money, I was a failure.

I started taking large, shaky steps of faith.

In the beginning, we received funds from a few successful businesspeople. It was a blessing, but they expected me to secure steady monthly support, something I had no idea how to do. When you're starting something new, people aren't always convinced you'll stick with it. They hold back, unsure whether your vision will last. There's always a long trial period before people begin to believe in the work and choose to give.

And then there was the awkward tension with our overseeing pastors from the U.S. They seemed to require loyalty I couldn't give. I couldn't give it because it was confusing and began to feel too controlling. They knew I needed finances but were not happy about my pursuing support for the homes. When I took in boys, they accused me of messing everything up and inviting kids from gangs into Nana's House. We needed a wide net of support—people from all over, not just one camp. But in their eyes, I was not capable, which made all those inferior feelings in me take over.

One time, the pastor's wife of our overseeing church in the U.S. invited me to speak at a women's event. I discussed the deep-seated brokenness our kids carry and how it manifests in raw, unpolished ways. But before I could get very far, she took the microphone out of my hand. No explanation. Just done.

I stood there stunned. I tried to be brave and asked bluntly if I had done something wrong. Silence. Before I left town to visit family nearby, I asked again—more silence. The third time I asked, I told them that if there was a problem, I wanted to know so I could rectify it. They told me to leave them alone. That was it.

I felt humiliated. And because these were our pastors—people who knew me well—it cut deep. I had never felt like I truly fit in or was enough for them. And now, it felt like bullying. I suffered from bullying for most of my childhood, but I wasn't about to stand down and walk away defeated this time. God had my back, and I would trust Him. He loved me, and He loved these kids.

I felt more driven than ever to raise the funds. God would have to come through, because I knew Nana's House was His idea and part of His plan.

A few days later, I traveled to Lewiston, Idaho, my dad's hometown and one of my favorite places. I went to visit my aunt and uncle, who lived a couple of hours away. When they invited me to speak at their church, I agreed, but I'll admit I felt intimidated. I still didn't fully understand what had happened at the previous church, and the memory lingered with me even as I said yes.

God would have to come through, because I knew Nana's House was His idea and part of His plan.

I remember walking alone along the Snake River, tears running down my face. I cried out to God. "What do You expect from me? I won't give up, but you have to help me. These kids need help. Please!"

The church in Idaho is called Granite Lake. My aunt

and uncle planted it when I was living with them during my high school years, so the church felt like family to me. It was a comfortable place to share, a place I felt welcomed by a lot of family and good friends.

The day, as I walked the path along the Snake River, I picked up the phone and started calling people I trusted—good, salt-of-the-earth people—and asked them to help support our orphanage, Nana's House, in Tepic, Mexico. Over time, I found people who really connected with Nana's House's vision. It wasn't easy, but peace began to return. Honestly, I made the resolve that no matter what happened, Nana's House would not only continue but also grow and become financially stable.

Pastor Chuck Gustafson in Oregon said yes; he just needed his board's approval. Then a dear friend in Alaska invited me to share at their church. I flew to Alaska, and that Sunday we raised $30,000 for Nana's House. It felt like a miracle. But the real challenge wasn't a one-time offering—it was building monthly support. Consistent, dependable help that could carry us month after month. That kind of stability didn't come quickly.

It took fourteen long years of pressing into God—year after year, holding tight to the vision and refusing to quit. We chose to stay the course, even during the violence and the worst type of chaos that plagued our town, trusting that God had our back. I stayed because the children of Nana's House had been abandoned, and I could never quit on them.

We, as a family, chose to stay even though there were so many reasons to leave. It wasn't easy at times, but God's grace was greater than our challenges, and His presence was with us even in the darkest valleys. We learned that sometimes the greatest act of faith is simply not leaving.

Chapter 4

Walking the Walk, Not the Stage

Over the years, I've learned that when I use words like "foster home" or "caring for children," people don't always grasp what we do. The word orphanage has an unattractive image attached to it, but that's what most people understand, so we use it. We are a nonprofit, and even though we are legally considered an orphanage, we function as a foster care home with government oversight, caring for children in dangerous situations, including those who have been trafficked and abused. The government offers many services that help kids in Mexico. They are a blessing but, we do not receive any government funding.

La Fuente Church, where my husband and I pastor, is a vital part of Nana's House. La Fuente is our spiritual covering and has been deeply woven into the life of the home. The children love the church and are actively involved—serving in nearby mission churches, participating in music and multimedia, helping in children's services, and some even working in our coffee shop. We consider La Fuente to be a significant reason for the success Nana's House has experienced.

The Nana's House team and I give our all. We're not perfect, but we're good at what we do. People often tell me, "What you do is amazing," and I'm grateful—but the truth is, I'm not the impressive, well-known speaker who draws big crowds or headlines. I'm not the polished face of an organization. I'm the one who knows every child's name, who sits with them when they cry, and who shows up in the middle of the chaos.

There are times when I wonder if being more "put together" or "important" would make it easier to raise the funds we need. Maybe doors would open faster if I fit that mold. But I've come to accept that my place is right here—on the ground, in Nana's House, surrounded by kids who have been through too much. It's not glamorous, but it's real. And that's where my heart is happiest.

We strive to create a true home for the children in our care. But imagine a group of adults trying to raise children together, united in purpose but with different backgrounds and personalities—it's not easy. Still, we've managed to make it work. Many of us have been here since the very beginning.

What I love most about Nana's House is the diversity of our team. Some of our staff hold university degrees, while others come from complex backgrounds. Many have found healing and transformation through their faith in Christ, and their lives are living testimonies of how deeply God can change a person. We are a big, imperfect family—loving kids who need that love.

To me, this place is beautiful chaos. It's full of intense moments, disagreements, and conflict, but it also overflows with love and a deep desire to see healing take place. We are family for those who want one.

We are a big, imperfect family— loving kids who need that love.

As a team, we've had to grow together, learning to let go of pride, refuse to take things personally, and stand firm in love. There's probably a disagreement every day, but it gets worked out. I've come to realize that when people bug me, I probably need to look at myself first.

Iron sharpens iron, and what kind of example would I be to the kids if I couldn't get along with the staff? I often need to step back and understand who I am dealing with. Does this issue need to be addressed, or am I being too picky? I'm the boss, but I like to work as a team.

Good character is essential as a leader, and as a team, we've had to recognize that we never stop learning, never stop growing, and never stop drawing close to God. If we do, problems will surely follow. We have to be secure in God's love before we can deal with kids who carry trauma.

Every child who comes to us has survived a nightmare of abuse and neglect. They arrive angry, broken-hearted, and often ready to fight. Our job is to stay grounded and not react. When a child lashes out, we don't engage in anger. We respond with calm: "Go to your room, cool off—we'll talk later." Why? Because many of these kids have never known a safe environment. They grew up outside the church, so cussing and hurling insults shaped how they talked. Life hurt them, abandoned them, and mistreated them, leaving scars in their words.

We believe discipline should come from a place of peace and love, not power or control. I've seen visitors shocked by the way a child might curse at a staff member. People who have observed this behavior would say, "Give me two weeks with that kid, and that behavior will stop." But it doesn't work that way. You can't just "fix" trauma overnight. Love, consistency, and patience—that's what works.

We've been doing this for eighteen years now. Over that time, we've witnessed countless stories—some full of redemption and hope, others with heartbreaking endings. But through it all, we remain present. We stay connected to the children we've cared for, continuing to pray for them and love them from afar.

They've changed us, too, and touched our hearts in ways we could never have imagined. As Psalm 34:18 says: "The Lord is close to the brokenhearted and saves those who are crushed in spirit." And that's precisely where we find Him—right here, in the middle of our beautiful chaos.

Their stories have changed the way I see God. Through their pain, resilience, and healing, I've come to understand more deeply God's commitment to love us. If my heart can burn with such passion to see these children and teens healed, it's only a faint reflection—a small fraction—of how fiercely God loves every one of us.

Eva's story is a great example. Her story and all the stories I share are why Nana's House exists.

Between the ages of four and eight, Eva was often left alone in her house for days at a time. There was rarely food. Her mother, lost in drug use, was emotionally checked out and frequently brought strange men home. Some of them abused Eva.

By the time she came to us, she had endured more trauma than most adults face in a lifetime. She was frightened, confused, and deeply wounded. We were still in our first year of running Nana's House, and honestly, I was unprepared for the pain this little girl carried.

Eva's fear often erupted as rage. She became violent and aggressive, lashing out at anyone who tried to get close. When she got upset, she'd back herself into a corner and grab anything within reach—a broom, a chair, whatever she could use to protect herself. She'd scream and cuss in Spanish, words I didn't understand at first. Let's just say by the end of that year, I had received quite the education in Spanish profanity.

Eventually, we realized we needed a dedicated space for kids to unwind—a place where they could let loose safely without disrupting the rest of the house. So, we created what we called the "meltdown room." It was small and cozy, with a giant stuffed animal in the center. The lighting was soft, the atmosphere calming. The door was a short, barn-style half-door, allowing us to always keep an eye on things, and one of us would sit quietly inside with the child, offering presence without pressure.

Years earlier, I had worked with children with autism, sitting with them after meltdowns, simply offering comfort. That experience helped guide how we cared for kids like Eva. Over time, we learned that calm voices and clear boundaries were far more effective than any form of punishment. When a child made a mess during an outburst, we waited until they calmed down, then gently asked them to clean it up—not to shame them, but to help them regain a sense of control and dignity.

Many of these children came from homes where the slightest mistake led to screaming, insults, or violence, so even a gentle correction could feel like a threat. A simple task could appear daunting. But once they realized we weren't going to hit, scream at, or shame them, they began to change. Slowly. But beautifully.

That's what happened with Eva.

Little by little, she discovered she was safe. And over the years, she learned how to live some peaceful moments. Eventually, a relative from another state stepped in, a family member who could offer her the kind of love and stability she deserved. And with time, Eva was able to leave us and step into a new, healing chapter of her life.

Most miracles don't happen beneath bright lights or on grand stages. They happen naturally, as life unfolds over time and we allow God to whisper His healing words. Most people never notice, but God is always there doing His most powerful, unseen work when no one else is watching.

Most miracles don't happen beneath bright lights or on grand stages.

I've always loved being with the girls. In the early years, every weekend, they spent time at my house. They loved—and still love—music and dancing. They would organize choreographed dances in my living room. They were mind-blowing in their dance moves, so natural and happy, and they made it look incredibly easy.

The girls who didn't dance instead did arts or baked in my kitchen with me. For a few years, we had a glorious tradition at Nana's House: We declared Saturdays as Exploring Days. That meant I'd pile all the girls into our trusty Pepto-Bismol colored van and head off to discover parts of places close to Tepic we'd never seen before. It sounded magical. It was magical—except for the times it wasn't.

For example, one weekend, we set our sights on Compostela, a charming little town known as a *Pueblo*

Mágico, which translates to "Magical Village"—though in our case the magic would turn...sour. The town boasts a beautiful lake, a peaceful walking trail, and delicious, fruity ice drinks that taste like heaven in a cup.

So far, so good.

We hiked around the lake, breathed in the fresh air, laughed a lot, and—of course—everyone got a fruity ice drink. It was the perfect day. Until we started driving home.

I had conveniently forgotten that the road back from Compostela is full of curves. Since many of our kids hadn't spent much time in vehicles before, that was a recipe for disaster.

About halfway home, one of the girls suddenly whispered, "I don't feel so good..."

Before I could respond—*bleh*. Right there in the van. No warning. No mercy.

But that was just the beginning. Like dominoes, one by one, the others started joining in. The smell, the sound, the splat. It was like a horrifying chain reaction. I was swerving around switchbacks with one hand on the wheel and the other hand trying to roll down windows while chanting to myself, *Don't you dare throw up, don't you dare throw up...*

But my gag reflex was alive and well. I was gagging and dry heaving and praying as if my life (or at least the contents of my stomach) depended on it.

By the time we pulled into Nana's House, the van smelled like a smoothie shop had exploded—and not in a good way.

Magical village? Maybe.

Magical mess? Without a doubt.

Magical memory? Absolutely.

To this day, though, the mere thought of fruity ice drinks still makes my stomach flip. Sour magic aside, I've found that what seems like a simple outing is really sacred time spent building memories that remind these kids they matter and that we're in this together. It's worth the mess.

In the early years, between 2008 and 2011, we were still living in the time of cartel wars, and my Nana's House kids were amazingly street-smart! I would drive around town and the little girls would say, "Hey, that car has no license plate, don't go near them." Other times, they would tell me, "Watch out, all those guys are covering their faces with knitted masks that the army often uses." They were very aware of their surroundings, and they sensed danger.

Several times in our neighborhood, Erika, who was the house mom at the time, and I found ourselves shouting to the kids, "Run upstairs! Hit the floor! Get under the bed!" The words felt foreign on our tongues, commands we never imagined we would have to give. One day, after barking out those instructions yet again, Erika and I locked eyes. A truck loaded with armed men had just rumbled past the front of Nana's House. In that moment, the weight of it all broke through, and we both burst into tears. Neither of us had ever dreamed life here would come to this.

Between the cartel war, the financial strain, and even dealing with violent girls at times, I found myself asking, *Am I crazy? Lord, how long do You expect me to keep doing this?*

God was molding my character and teaching me to trust Him, but under the circumstances, this was not an easy task. I knew one thing: I could not do this without God. I was very dependent on Him. I was just walking, trusting God, and doing the things nobody could see. There was no glamor, no spotlight, and not much thanks, but I was happy. Deep down, I knew I was right where I was supposed to be, doing what mattered most, even if no one else noticed. Most of life is walking the walk, and nobody notices the small, unseen steps that, together, make it beautifully real.

Chapter 5

Stepping Into the Fear I Tried to Run From

I never wanted to be a fundraiser, but to keep Nana's House going, I had no choice—nobody else was doing it. Life has a way of giving you lessons disguised as "easy" tasks. People told me two things would be simple for me: learning a language and raising funds. They assured me I'd be fluent in Spanish within a year, which turned out to be far from the truth. And fundraising? They said, "Once people hear what you're doing, they'll give—easy-peasy." If only it were that simple.

When I had the opportunity to travel and raise funds for the orphanage, I'd often run into people eager to tell me about their favorite orphanage, which was usually some massive operation overseas caring for thousands of children. And I get it—that's impressive.

But my max was thirty.

There were thirty kids whose names I knew by heart. We celebrated thirty birthdays with cake, gifts, and laughter. We rushed thirty kids to the doctor when they were sick. Thirty kids celebrated Christmas with lots of dancing, singing, and breaking piñatas, creating memories that would last a lifetime.

No, we didn't have thousands. But we had—and still have—something powerful: the gift of speaking their language and truly reaching their hearts.

What we're doing might not look impressive on paper, but don't let that fool you. It's real. And it's deeply personal. We're not building a brand or chasing applause. We're building lives, one moment of trust at a time.

Nana's House isn't about numbers—it's about names. It's about kids who had nowhere safe to go, no one to trust, and no reason to believe life could ever get better. Until now.

My job and my calling are to communicate the fierce, tender love God has for these children. And for some reason, He decided to share that love with us, allowing us to be part of it. That love looks like a thousand small things: showing up, sharing the love God placed in our hearts for these children.

Let me be honest—raising money for a nonprofit is no joke. It's exhausting. It's humbling. And sometimes it feels like I'm shouting into the wind, hoping someone hears me. But we keep going. We keep asking because these kids are worth it.

Every dollar that comes in? That's another child with a chance, another young person learning what safety feels like, another step toward healing. Every single "yes" from a donor becomes part of a story of hope.

People sometimes ask how we keep going. And the answer is simple: love. Not the easy kind, but the kind that stays. The kind that fights. The kind that believes in people even when they're falling apart. The kind that Jesus lived and died for. We're just trying to follow His example.

So, yes, this work may seem small to some. But from where I'm standing, it's a miracle unfolding, one life at a time.

I have nothing against mega ministries that support thousands of children—in fact, I admire them. They're doing incredible work. They're awe-inspiring. But my calling is different.

My calling is to connect deeply with these kids. To know their names, their stories, and the secret hopes they carry in their hearts. To notice when something's wrong just by the look in their eyes. To celebrate their victories, big and small, and to walk with them through the valleys.

Their stories deserve to be told. My voice is for kids who matter, and I'm determined to keep using it.

And to do that well—to truly show up for them in every way—I must limit how many children we can take in at a time.

We may not have thousands in our care. But the ones we do have, we love dearly. We're building relationships that last a lifetime. We are not just providing food—we are creating a family, a place where these kids know they belong, where their hearts can heal, and where their dreams can grow.

My husband is a gifted preacher and, when needed, a skilled fundraiser. He does both things with ease and grace.

But when I realized that I would have to travel to raise funds—that I would be the one speaking, sharing in churches, and standing before rooms full of strangers—I was nervous. I had never pictured myself in that role. The thought of public speaking used to make my knees shake.

But here's the surprising part: once I started, I discovered that I actually enjoyed it. Well, I enjoyed the sharing part. Telling people about the children, the stories, the miracles, and even the struggles—that part came naturally to me.

Still, there was a challenge. For some churches, the idea of a woman traveling alone—without her husband—felt uncomfortable. Even suspicious. Years ago, my husband and I decided to take turns traveling, unless it was for family vacations or intentional time together. There were several reasons behind this choice, but mainly it came down to focus and finances. When one of us traveled for ministry, we wanted our full attention to be on what God had called us to do during that trip. I was trying to raise funds, not pay double the cost of my journey.

Being a woman seemed, at times, to work against me. While I formed great friendships with several churches that welcomed me and gave me freedom to share, there were many others where I felt held at a distance. They didn't allow me to speak freely. They only wanted to interview me during the church service. They didn't permit me to step onto the platform alone. Someone else needed to hold the microphone, as if my voice somehow had to be managed.

It was discouraging because I'm good at telling stories. And it made it hard for me to share the way I knew I could—the way God called me to share.

I've lost count of the trips that left me frustrated and in tears, feeling the weight of resistance that was difficult to name but impossible to ignore. And if I'm honest, I know much of it came to one simple fact: I'm a woman.

But here's what I've learned: God called me, not only my husband. And no matter how many obstacles I faced, I kept going because the kids are worth it. Because their stories deserve to be told. My voice is for kids who matter, and I'm determined to keep using it.

I had to let go of the fear and face a lot of things I wanted to run from. Once I did, I learned so much about myself.

One of the lowest moments of my life came at a conference several years ago. We were right in the middle of the sessions when my husband pulled me aside and quietly told me we had zero funds left for Nana's House. Just like that, our Nana's House budget was gone.

I felt like someone had punched me in the gut.

And as if that weren't enough, I stood there, observing the prominent leaders at the conference treating my husband with thinly veiled condescension that made my blood boil. There's this undercurrent you sense at these gatherings on occasion—a subtle competition to prove whose ministry is the biggest, the most successful, the worthiest of attention. And that atmosphere drives me crazy.

And to top it all off, a well-known leader—someone who knew exactly what we were doing—introduced me to his friends like this: "She's doing something… with kids…"

I stood there, stunned. The leader wasn't confused. He knew our work. But in that moment, it felt dismissed—like Nana's House wasn't even worth naming.

I was so upset I could barely manage a polite smile. I remember excusing myself and going outside just to calm down and breathe. Looking back, I wish I hadn't let things like that get under my skin. I tell myself I should have been more secure, but the truth is that money has always been a significant issue for me, and you can't run an orphanage without it. There were staff salaries to cover, rent to pay, and endless needs for the kids.

A damaged ego can become a monster.

I took a very long walk. I was practically talking out loud as I prayed, my voice shaking with frustration.

"God, are You there? What am I supposed to do? I can't see a way forward. What's the plan?"

I felt like God whispered in my ear: "Do you want to quit?"

The question startled me. I stopped walking and stood there for a moment, really letting it sink in.

"No, I don't want to quit. No, I'm not quitting."

I said it out loud, my voice sharp, like I was daring the universe to challenge me. "I love these kids with every ounce of my being. I will not give up." Then, softer but no less desperate, "God... I don't know how to keep going."

But deep in my gut, I already knew—money or no money, we'd make it work. Because you don't let go of kids who've already been tossed aside by the very people who were supposed to fight for them. You don't back away when a child's heart is smashed into a thousand jagged pieces, scattered so far you don't have any idea how to piece it back together. And you sure don't abandon a child who's already been crushed under the weight of being abandoned once. Not on my watch.

Even if no one ever remembered what I did—even if I never had a place on the big stage and the funds completely dried up—I knew my purpose. I wasn't in this to impress anyone.

I had taken on a lot, but God knew, and I chose to trust Him. Everything in me said, *Keep marching forward.*

In the process, I was learning to lean on God in my insecurities. And it wasn't just me—the children, my staff, all of us were growing in Him. Nana's House has not only transformed the lives of children, but also the lives of so many who have come through its doors, and even those who are still with us today.

My insecurities often cause me to turn inward, relying on my own strength instead of leaning on Jesus. My goal is to be more like Jesus. But sometimes, my ego gets in the way. I've come to realize that insecurity is often just another face of ego. It's easy to think of ego as arrogance or pride, but sometimes it shows up as fear, self-doubt, and a constant craving for validation. My damaged ego had grown far more significant in my mind than I ever wanted to admit.

A damaged ego can become a monster. It twists the way I see the world, distorting even small slights into deep wounds, making me obsess over how others perceive me, how my ministry measures up, or whether people truly understand or value what I'm doing. It turns every moment into a scorecard, every conversation into a hidden competition.

My ego wanted to scream, to defend myself, to prove my worth. To ensure people understood the sacrifices I was making and the effort I was putting in.

But I was learning a painful truth: that my insecurity—and my damaged ego—had to be laid aside and silenced if I was ever going to keep moving forward in faith.

God wasn't just using me to rescue kids—He was rescuing me too. Every step of this journey has exposed something inside me that needed healing. To do what I do, I had to face so many fears. And as I faced them, I began to realize that most of my worries weren't about circumstances at all; they were about trust. God was teaching me to trust Him completely, even when I felt unqualified or afraid. In helping these children find freedom, He was setting me free too.

So, I had to keep reminding myself that God sees what no one else sees. He understands the battles we fight. He knows the tears we cry. And He's the One who provides—not me, not the donors, not the people on the big conference stages.

I had to choose to trust that even if I felt unseen, unheard, or undervalued, God hadn't forgotten me or the kids.

Faith meant letting go of my need to control how people saw me. It meant releasing my grip on my damaged ego and choosing to believe that God would provide, even when the bank account screamed otherwise.

It's still a journey. Some days, my ego tries to claw its way back into the driver's seat. But I keep bringing it to Jesus. Because I want to be like Him—a servant, humble and secure in the Father's love. When I'm weak, He's strong. And somehow, that's enough.

> "Who, being in very nature God,
> Did not consider equality with God something to be used to his own advantage;
> Rather, he made himself nothing
> By taking the very nature of a servant,
> Being made in human likeness.
> And being found in appearance as a man,
> he humbled himself
> By becoming obedient to death—
> Even death on a cross!"
> (Philippians 2:6–8)

I know plenty of people who shine at self-promotion, who seem born to stand in the spotlight. But I'm simply not one of them. I never have been, and I doubt I ever will be. For me, it's God or nothing. Without Him, this whole thing would have sunk to the bottom a long time ago. I need faith like oxygen. I need God's provision.

So, I keep going—not because I'm craving recognition or applause, but because there are children and teens out there who desperately need someone who doesn't need to be the center of the world.

They need stability. They need safety. They need a place to belong, a place to call home.

And if God can use me, with all my flaws and fears, to help provide that, then I'm all in.

I once heard that the best thing you can do for yourself is to do the things you don't want to do. For me, fundraising is precisely that. It's challenging, uncomfortable, and often the last thing I want to face. Yet it keeps me focused, keeps me moving, and somehow, when I speak or write about our work, support comes in. It's a challenge I didn't ask for, but in the end, it's one that God has blessed. And for that, I'm grateful.

Chapter 6

Purpose in the Chaos

I could say I have a gift to see purpose in chaotic moments, and I think it's biblical. Jesus allowed chaos and even led His disciples into a storm (the storm on the sea in Mark 4:35–41). He led His disciples into the storm, not around it, and then calmed it with a word. I chose a life lived on the edge of a continual storm, knowing God was going to bring peace and calm the waves.

We live in a subtropical area, where summer rains last for nearly five months each year. During those storms, the streets turn into rivers, trees fall, and the sky seems to open. Thankfully, we're usually spared from a direct hurricane hit, though we often get what we call the tail—the outer winds and heavy rains that still pack quite a punch.

One year, a big storm rolled through. I decided to stay the night at Nana's House to help, knowing the first thing to go would likely be the electricity. I wanted to be close in case something went wrong. We had a bit of construction underway, and someone left several large sheets of metal stacked on the grounds. I worried they might take flight and hurt someone passing by.

So, I went out into the storm to weigh them down. An older teen came with me, and together we did our best to secure everything. Just as we finished, a strong gust of wind hit me square in the back, sending me flying into an enormous patch of mud. I looked like a swamp creature—completely covered, sticky from head to toe, and laughing in disbelief at the mess.

Later that night, as the wind howled outside, I realized that ministry—and life with God—is often like that storm.

Even in the chaos, God is present. It's unpredictable and messy, and sometimes it knocks you flat on your back. But even in the chaos, God is present. He doesn't always calm the storm right away; sometimes He just teaches us to find peace and purpose in the middle of it.

I believe that everything I experienced growing up with a mother who had deep emotional struggles prepared me for the work I do with children today. God used my difficult, stormy childhood to give me patience and purpose to help kids who struggle with rage.

Those early years taught me how to hold steady when emotions run wild. With some of the kids I work with, their pain is so raw, so overwhelming, that it can feel almost like confronting a demon. Yet because of what I've lived through, I've learned to face that intensity with compassion. I can meet them in their fear and help them feel safe enough to hopefully begin healing. I think all of us who work in Nana's House can say our past doesn't define us, but it has given us the courage and empathy to walk alongside children through the darkest parts of their own stories.

In 2011, I received a call that stopped me in my tracks. It was Child Protective Services. A young boy—just ten years old—had tried to take his own life.

I already had three of his sisters living in Nana's House, and I had a long, tangled history with their mother. When they asked me if I could take him in, my heart screamed yes—but my mind reeled. We didn't even have a boys' home. We were barely making ends meet with the girls' home.

I could feel the walls closing in. I'd been told, "Don't take on anything more," but my husband was out of town, and as for the overseeing pastors from the U.S., I hoped they would trust I made the right decision.

It was just my team and me, standing in the middle of it all, feeling the weight of the impossible. The risks weighed heavy. The reasons to say no grew louder. The safe thing would have been to walk away. But how do you walk away from a ten-year-old boy who had tried to die?

So, I said yes. We opened a boys' home.

All I knew was that I couldn't ignore the ache to give that boy a chance at life.

Francisco had been in the hospital for ten days. The nurses had called CPS after noticing how tense and withdrawn he became when his mother was nearby. She had pushed him to help pay rent, sending him to the streets to beg for money or steal food. He was just a child, carrying the weight of survival on his small shoulders. One day, it became too heavy. He took a bottle of his mother's pills, hoping to escape the pain forever.

I couldn't ignore the ache to give that boy a chance at life.

When Francisco came to us, his eyes were storm clouds—dark, unpredictable, ready to erupt at the slightest spark. He spent one whole day screaming for help at the top of his lungs. He got so angry one day that he destroyed a sink and locked himself in the bathroom. He often threatened to hurt one of us, but it was always just a threat, and he never hurt anyone.

Trauma clung to him like a second skin. On good days, he could laugh, even relax. On bad days, rage poured out of him like lava, destructive, unstoppable.

We set firm but gentle boundaries. Chaos was familiar to him, but safety was not. He didn't know how to trust calm. As he grew older, I could see he wanted to do better, but the anger ran deep. His rages grew stronger, but so did the flickers of hope.

I'll never forget the day he stood in his doorway, drenched in sweat, screaming, "Help me!" He wasn't defiant—he was tormented.

We took him to psychiatrists and psychologists. The medication dulled the edge, therapy helped a little, but the storms always came back. We learned to ride them out. To wait through the fury until the calm returned and he would collapse in our arms, sobbing, exhausted, torn between wanting comfort and being terrified to trust it.

So, we held on. He was worth fighting for.

Eventually, Francisco grew up enough to step out into the world. He was stronger and steadier, but I knew there were wounds still not healed. Some scars run deeper than time—or even love—can reach. He carried pieces of his past with him, pain that hid just under the surface.

Healing isn't a straight line. His story taught me that sometimes, just staying in the fight is the victory. Sometimes purpose hides in the blur of chaos, only coming into focus when time and grace reveal it. Often, God asks us to walk into chaos because that's where purpose is waiting.

Jesus did the same. He wasn't the Savior anyone expected. His path led straight into danger and, eventually, the cross. It didn't make sense to those watching, but it was the only way redemption could come.

I knew I was inviting chaos into my life when I took on Nana's House, but my heart burned with a passion to help children trapped in heartbreaking circumstances. Years later, I look back, almost shocked at how bold I was. It was a mixture of courage and considerable stress. But in the middle of it all, I was learning so much about God's love.

There was certainly chaos, but God was shaping me and the staff. We were walking a road that would lead to a kind of chaos that gives birth to extraordinary things. Many people with broken hearts are like works of art—complex, layered, and stunning in their own unique way. Time after time, we've seen the beauty hidden in the complexity of the children under our care.

Since then, Francisco has studied, worked hard, and held steady jobs. On the outside, his life looks strong and stable, and in many ways, it is. But I know that peace does not come easily for him. It is something he has had to wrestle with, one day at a time. And yet, even with the storms he has faced within, he is one of the kindest people you could ever meet. His heart is gentle, his words are thoughtful, and his loyalty runs deep.

He truly loves us, and we love him in return. Our bond has never been broken, even when life took him down roads that pulled him far from us. He will always be part of our family, no matter the distance or the years. To this day, he remains in our prayers—lifted with hope, covered with faith, and wrapped in love. Taking in Francisco and starting the boys' home was walking into chaos with a purpose and choosing a risky path. And, in the end, I can see Jesus leading me into the storm, trusting that He would calm it and bring peace.

When it comes to finding purpose in chaos, it's important to realize this purpose might not look like what you originally expected. When we started Nana's House, I had an idealized, less-messy picture of what it would become, and it's taken many years to understand that true purpose often lies beneath the surface.

One of the biggest expectations I had to adjust was my idea that Nana's House would immediately feel like a "real home" to all the kids. I wanted the children to feel loved, secure, and safe—as though they truly belonged. And in my mind, that translated to everyone fitting in quickly and understanding how families operate.

It sounds excellent, and for years, I believed that creating that atmosphere was the ultimate goal. But to be honest, it's often hard to admit when the ideal and the reality are at odds—and sometimes, they simply clash. What we were doing was good and deeply meaningful, but these children come from incredibly problematic backgrounds. They're taken away from everything they've ever known and brought to a place that's supposed to be "home," yet it's a home they've never experienced before. Expecting them to simply accept us as family, or to immediately adjust to our way of doing things, was a far bigger battle than I ever imagined.

I wanted the children to feel loved, secure, and safe—as though they truly belonged.

I used to think it would be almost magical—that they'd naturally appreciate a tidy home and all the comforts we offered. However, that idea turned out to be much more unrealistic than I had realized.

Many of the kids who come to us have never even slept in a bed; they prefer sleeping on the floor because it feels familiar and safe. Some are unaware of the purpose of a sheet or pillowcase. The sheet situation alone can be a challenge. Often, the kids want to sleep directly on the mattress. I find myself explaining over and over that while you can wash a sheet, cleaning a mattress isn't so easy. "So please," I tell them gently, "use the sheet."

Housework is another area where we have to start from scratch. Many children have no idea how to fold clothes—or that you're even supposed to fold clothes—and the concept of washing your own plate after eating is utterly foreign to them. We have to teach them how to use a broom and a mop without turning the whole activity into a comedy show.

And then there's the washing machine. If the kids are old enough, we show them how to run it, which sounds simple enough until you've lived through the "laundry disasters." Let me tell you, I could fill an entire book just with stories about soap suds creeping across the floor like an invading army, shirts dyed wild colors because someone snuck a bright red sock into the load, or the time a child tried to wash their shoes and their stuffed animals together because, well, "They were both dirty."

We laugh (eventually), but it's all part of teaching them life skills—and collecting a few funny stories along the way.

Thankfully, the women who work at Nana's House are magnificent cooks, and they teach the older girls how to cook as well, which is a skill that will bless them for the rest of their lives. Over in our boys' home, the leader, Hugo, is also a great cook and takes the time to teach the boys how to prepare meals.

Despite the delicious food, many kids come to us accustomed to only a few simple things—such as quesadillas or tortas—and they're hesitant to try new dishes. I made a rule early on not to fight with them over food. Instead, I give them time to adjust and discover new flavors at their own pace. So far, nobody has starved. The ladies are afraid that if they don't eat the excellent food they made, the child will starve, but that has never happened and never will happen.

These children have lived with trauma for most of their lives. And the day they're brought to Nana's House is often one of the most traumatic moments of all. They're being taken away from the only world they've ever known—even if that world was painful.

Nana's House is a special place, but not every child who comes through our doors will immediately appreciate what we have to offer. Expecting them to feel like family right away, or to adjust as easily as a middle-class child who's always known warm meals, sheets on their bed, and a tidy home, is simply not fair to them.

We're learning, day by day, to meet them where they are and help them discover what a safe and loving home can genuinely be.

Sometimes love leads us to create chaos with purpose. Scripture is one crazy situation after another—storms, failures, miracles, and second chances—but none of it is random. It leads us to see that God is love.

Purpose in chaos rarely arrives wrapped in clarity or comfort. Instead, it shows up as faithfulness in the mess, patience in the process, and love that never fails. When we meet people where they are and refuse to abandon them in the storm, we often discover that God has been shaping something beautiful there all along.

Chapter 7

God's Grace Is Always Generous

God's grace allows us to serve without expecting any-thing in return. His grace is always available, even when some children struggle to accept it. But we know that once they experience His love and grace, it becomes something they can carry with them—something that will never leave, no matter what. Girls who have lived through trafficking rarely share their pasts, and we honor their silence. It's important to understand that being traf-ficked does not always mean being kidnapped or forced into prostitution. Most traffickers groom, manipulate, and abuse girls over time, and that ongoing abuse eventually draws them into trafficking.

At Nana's House, we see the resilience and strength of these children. Even in a few short words or moments, we come to understand the depth of their experiences.

At Nana's House, we see the resilience and strength of these children.

Their stories shine a light on a harsh reality—not just in Mexico, but across the world. Young girls, some as young as ten, are sold to men, stripped of their childhoods and innocence. And the truth is, it's not only girls; boys are trafficked as well. It's a tragedy that defies easy words, yet sharing even glimpses of these stories helps people see the urgent need for awareness, compassion, and action.

Here is the story of Abby. Every child's story is the reason Nana's House exists. We are here for teens like Abby.

Abby was sent to us a few years ago, and she arrived with bruises all over her body, each one a silent witness to the battles she'd fought in her young life. She carried herself with a tough veneer, her eyes sharp and guarded, as if daring anyone to get too close. She was a beautiful young lady, polite enough at first, but there was a constant tension simmering just under the surface.

One day, I pulled her aside and gently asked her to tell me about her life. She hesitated, her gaze shifting away. Finally, she admitted she'd run away from her very abusive home and had been working in a bar. I asked her what she did there, and suddenly she fell silent, her jaw tightening as she stared at the floor.

After a long, heavy silence, she finally spoke, her voice barely above a whisper. "Men bought me drinks."

That was all she needed to say. I knew exactly what that meant. Men had sexually abused Abby when she was a child, and now she was living with the scars. She had survived the only way she knew—by selling herself. And even though she was underage, the place that had taken her in had trafficked girls like Abby. She couldn't say the rest. Or maybe she wouldn't. Either way, she didn't have to. The pain behind her eyes said everything.

Despite everything, Abby was brilliant. She managed to finish junior high with us quickly, still clinging to her rough attitude, though I could see flashes of softness creeping in. God's grace was there for her. But behind her eyes was a constant question: *Why do you like me? Why do you trust me?*

She couldn't hold onto the grace because something told her she was not good enough. She didn't understand that we trusted her. She saw the grace of God in so many ways at Nana's House, which is why I say God's grace is generous, but we have to accept it to experience it.

She couldn't comprehend that we genuinely did like her. She was, quite simply, a very likable young woman.

We enrolled her in high school and a nail technician course. Things seemed to be going well on the surface. But then cracks began to appear. Abby started getting defensive over the most minor things, insisting we didn't trust her. One day, I asked her a simple question, and she exploded in anger, as if I'd accused her of something terrible.

Then, without warning, she left for high school one morning and never came back. My heart sank as we reported her as a runaway, clinging to hope that she was safe yet fearing the worst. Months later, the call came. The police had found her—but not the way we had prayed for. Abby was in the red-light district, drugged, numb, and selling herself just to survive. The police hadn't even been looking for her; they were after someone else when they stumbled across her.

I've heard she's living with some of her family now. And occasionally, she slips into the back row of our church because she experienced the grace of God, and that type of grace sticks with you. I'm so happy she shows up; her presence alone is a miracle to me.

There is still hope for Abby. Her story isn't over. We carry her in our hearts, and we love her just as she is.

In Mexico and all over the world, countless children face the painful reality of abandonment. Some are left on the streets because of poverty, substance abuse, family violence, mental health issues, or the breakdown of social support systems. The consequences of this abandonment are profound, affecting every part of a child's life.

We've taken in kids who, even at twelve years old, have never set foot in a classroom. Thankfully, with the proper support, many can catch up within just a few years. That's why we always hope they'll stay with us long enough to reach grade level.

I remember a young girl named Greta, whom we took in many years ago. Her father, after his wife left him, began claiming his daughter as his wife and treating her as such. She had never been to school and carried deep wounds from the trauma she endured.

When Greta arrived, she was withdrawn and afraid. It took time, patience, and a great deal of love for her to begin trusting again. She went through a long journey of emotional healing, with counseling, support from our staff, and the safety of a stable environment, helping her reclaim her sense of self-worth. She was willing to open her heart to God and to us. She was willing to grasp the grace we offered her.

Through our government-authorized school program, she managed to catch up academically. She eventually went on to college and graduated, and today she's an excellent pastry chef. Her resilience and determination are nothing short of inspiring, a powerful reminder that with the proper care and opportunities, even the deepest wounds can begin to heal.

Education is at the heart of what we do at Nana's House. It is more than learning facts or skills—it is a key to freedom. Education teaches children to think for themselves, to question, and to imagine a life beyond the limitations placed on them. It shows them they don't have to depend on others; they can make choices, pursue their dreams, and build a life of their own. Through education, we help them reclaim the power and hope that every child deserves.

Education teaches children to think for themselves, to question, and to imagine a life beyond the limitations placed on them.

We run a school for the children in Nana's House until they reach high school. I usually get excited when a child makes it to high school. Most kids do very well, but sometimes it's challenging to help a teenager navigate high school.

We have many high school graduates, and every diploma feels like a hard-won victory because the stakes are painfully high. For those who manage to graduate, there's a strong chance they'll go on to college and carve out a better future.

Some of the kids who leave are incredibly bright. School comes easily to them, and it breaks my heart to see them waste all that potential. More than academics, it's a daily battle against wounds from their past. Against fear, shame, and the voices in their heads that tell them they'll never be anything more than what life has already dealt them.

I remember one young man who was—and still is—brilliant. He graduated from high school with top grades. But underneath the good reports and polite smile, there were warning signs. He started smoking pot, chasing girls, and becoming increasingly passive-aggressive about the rules.

One day, I found drugs hidden in his room. My heart dropped into my stomach. I knew what that path could lead to, and I also knew I couldn't keep him at Nana's House any longer. It wouldn't be safe for him or the others. It was one of those moments that rips your soul in two because you care about them so deeply, but you also have to protect the whole house.

Thankfully, a wonderful couple from our church stepped in and took him under their wing. We stayed in close contact, refusing to give up on him. He kept attending church, learned how to garden, and even started a small gardening business. Slowly, bit by bit, he began to believe he was capable of something better. We were always there for him.

Then, one day, he told us he wanted to enroll in our Bible school. I could hardly believe it. It was like watching someone emerge from a dark tunnel into the sunlight. He had held onto a grace he knew was real in the end. Today, he's an intern at one of our churches—a living testimony that even when darkness tries to pull them under, hope can still prevail. He is enrolling in the university to study architecture. God's grace was always on him; he just needed to feel it for himself.

These stories keep me going. But they also remind me that every day, we're fighting a genuine and relentless battle for the lives and futures of these kids.

Once, a lady looked me straight in the eyes and told me that the kids I take in will never succeed. That for generations, their families have known nothing but failure, and nothing would ever change. Her words cut deep, igniting both anger and sorrow in me, because I refuse to believe that any child's future has to be chained to the past.

At Nana's House, we embrace and fight for the least likely to succeed, because we, too, carry stories that once screamed, "No hope!" Yet the love of God rewrote our destinies—and we believe with all our hearts that His love can transform every child's story into one of victory and light.

If we are truly followers of Jesus, we will fight for the forgotten, for the overlooked, for the "least likely to succeed." Jesus said, "Truly I tell you, whatever you did for one of the least of these brothers and sisters of mine, you did for me" (Matthew 25:40).

In that passage, "the least of these" refers to those who are hungry, thirsty, strangers, naked, sick, or in prison. Jesus identifies Himself radically with those who suffer. Serving them is serving Him.

Jesus was constantly moving toward the margins— toward the poor, the sick, the outcast, the sinful, the powerless. His message flipped society's values upside down. He wasn't impressed by wealth, power, or religious status. He cared about the forgotten, the broken, the marginalized.

When we care for widows, orphans, and the most vulnerable, we echo Jesus' mission. James 1:27 ties this directly to genuine faith: "Religion that God our Father accepts as pure and faultless is this: to look after orphans and widows in their distress and to keep oneself from being polluted by the world."

I believe I have a gift in being merciful, and in Jesus, that gift is good; but in my flesh, it can cause misery because I ended up carrying too much on my shoulders. Only God's love can repair deep brokenness.

Only God's love can repair deep brokenness. One time we took in a young girl from a nearby beach town known as the Tree Girl. Her real name was Camila. She slept in the branches of trees, hidden away, probably because it was safer than the world on the ground. Safer than the hands meant to protect her.

Camila was eight years old when she arrived at our door. From the very beginning, we could feel the storm raging inside her. She had no impulse control; one day, when we were going to the park, she tried to jump out of a moving car.

Part of me knew right then that this might be too much for us. But how do you turn away a child who sleeps in trees to escape monsters in her own home? How do you say, "No, you're too broken for us to love"? So we didn't say no.

Instead, we said yes. We brought Camila in, determined that love could heal anything, that Jesus could reach even the deepest wounds. We threw everything we had into helping her. We worked with professionals, searched for answers, and prayed until our voices were hoarse.

But as Camila grew older, the violence grew with her. Her tantrums became terrifying storms. She would hit anyone who came too close to her. The house trembled under the weight of her anger and outbursts. The other children began living in fear. They'd watch Camila out of the corners of their eyes, waiting for the explosion.

She even attacked neighbors. I'm convinced she had brain damage because nothing worked—no pill, hours of counseling, living in a place that loved her—nothing. We took her to specialists, but the type of test she needed was out of our price range; we simply didn't have the thousands of dollars required.

It was killing me inside. I loved Camila, but I was watching the rest of the children pay a price they shouldn't have to pay. No child should live afraid in a house meant to be safe.

I wrestled with the decision for months, my heart breaking either way. But the day came when I knew: We couldn't keep her anymore. She had been with us for six years.

We took her to a psychiatrist at the local public hospital, still clinging to hope that someone might unlock the mystery of her pain. Maybe there'd be a medication, a therapy, a miracle.

But in the middle of talking to the doctor, Camila exploded. One moment, she was staring into space; the next, she swung her arm with her fist and punched me in the nose with all her strength. My glasses flew off, skittering across the floor.

Before I could move, Camila vaulted onto the doctor's desk, knocking over files and scattering pens and paper. She seized the doctor's computer, shrieking, trying to yank it off the desk, her face twisted in rage.

We screamed for the police officer outside. He rushed in, wrestled Camila down, and pinned her while she fought like a cornered animal.

We called Child Protective Services. "We can't do this anymore. We can't keep Camila in Nana's House." It felt like I was betraying her. But I knew we'd reached the end.

The story hit the newspapers. And it wouldn't be the last time we were in the newspaper. Years later, we heard from Camila. We know she is being cared for by others in her hometown, and we hope and pray that she is holding onto the grace of God, who never lets go of her.

Sometimes, healing requires a choice—to see and receive God's love and mercy—and we continue to pray that she makes that choice. Through cases like Camila's, I've learned that mercy, as beautiful as it is, often works subtly, slowly, and with patience. It reminds me that God's love reaches even the places we cannot, and that hope is never lost.

I had to learn to let certain situations go, to lay down the weight I was never meant to carry, and to lean on God and His perfect mercy. I had to learn to rest in His strength instead of my own.

We've faced some tough cases since Camila. But we've also learned a great deal. We've become wiser about what we can handle and when to seek help. Child Protective Services in Mexico has also changed, and mental health care has improved significantly over the years.

Together as a team, we're able to navigate things better now. We know we're not alone. We've learned to trust God not only to rescue the most desperate children but also to care for the quiet ones who wait patiently for someone to see them.

And I'm still learning, every day, how to hold mercy in my hands without letting it crush me. How to love deeply and yet know my limits, how to trust that God's mercy reaches farther than mine ever could.

All we can do once they leave is pray and trust that the grace they once touched, even for a time, is still holding them. For the children who feel invisible or unloved, God's grace is the steady presence that says, "You matter. You are seen. You are mine." It is unshakable, unending, and always available. No matter how far we've fallen or how lost we feel, God's grace is always there.

Some children don't heal the way we pray they will. Some walk away still carrying pain. Grace doesn't always land where we hope it will. It doesn't always change the story the way we want.

But I know it still holds them. *God* holds them. He holds them when all we can do is pray and trust that His mercy reaches farther than our arms ever could.

Chapter 8

Where Laughter Lives

A buse steals childhoods. At Nana's House, we work to restore it by creating a place where kids feel safe, loved, and truly accepted.

For four unforgettable years, Nana's House was right next door to mine. Back then, we were renting, and the house pulsed with laughter, tears, and the rhythms of daily life. Erika was our house mom during those years—a perfect fit for the chaos and beauty that is Nana's House. She had a gift for creating order out of chaos, establishing routines and traditions that we still follow today.

One of the best parts of having Nana's House so close was how often the girls would pop over. My home was like an extension of theirs, filled with spontaneous dance parties, movie nights, and shared meals that over-flowed with giggles and the scent of home-cooked food.

As Nana's House grew, so did our need for space. The little house next door was bursting at the seams, so we rented a bigger place near our church. The new home was a quirky one, full of odd angles and funky charm, but it worked beautifully—mainly because of the huge patio where the girls could run, play, and just be kids.

As Nana's House grew, so did our need for space.

With the extra space, we were able to welcome more girls. They still walked to my house regularly, keeping our tradition of meals together, sleepovers, dance time, and movie marathons. Those were sweet, precious times.

I had been in full-time ministry since I was twenty-two, and by the time I opened Nana's House, I was forty-seven. My passion for this work burned bright, even in the most challenging moments when exhaustion whispered that I should quit. When you see children arrive heavy with sadness—and then hear their laughter, watch them play, or even get into a bit of mischief—it's one of the most rewarding experiences in life.

We rented a house in the heart of a large neighbor-hood, and the girls' bedrooms all faced the street. It wasn't long before we noticed a curious pattern: Groups of young boys were riding their bikes past the house often.

It turned out the girls had invented a covert communication network. They were dropping little love notes out the windows to the boys below as they zoomed by on their bikes, blowing kisses from the second floor like starlets in a romantic movie. Before we knew it, drama erupted. The girls were suddenly fighting over boys they barely even knew, and we were stunned to discover they'd been carrying on an entire secret social life from their bedroom windows.

As if that weren't enough, they were also delighting in squirting unsuspecting pedestrians with water guns from behind curtains and collapsing into fits of giggles.

But our nighttime troubles were the real kicker. We couldn't get the girls to sleep—especially when a particular lady was on duty in the house. No matter how hard she tried, the girls kept up noise and shenanigans until the wee hours.

Determined to crack the mystery, I decided to sleep over one night to observe. At first, the girls were quiet as mice. I thought perhaps my reputation for being firm had intimidated them…until I heard the giggling.

Sure enough, when I peeked in, I found two of the girls sitting in the middle of the room, a giant toy chest dragged out, and an elaborate tea party in full swing. Dolls were propped up, sipping invisible tea. Honestly, it was so impressive I got the giggles myself. I had to gather my seriousness, tell them it was time for bed, and crawl back under my blanket before I cracked up again.

Unfortunately, my one-night stay didn't resolve the issue. When the other lady returned for her shift, the girls resumed their noisy ways, keeping her awake for hours each night.

So, I devised a little plan. I told the staff member not to worry because I'd be there bright and early. And I meant *early*.

At 5:30 a.m., I arrived armed with pots and metal spoons, clanging away like a one-woman marching band. The racket echoed through the house, startling all the girls awake.

They were half-shocked and half-impressed—but they got the message: There are hours for noise, and there are hours when everyone needs to sleep.

And yes—we all had a good laugh about it afterward.

Children need to be children and not carry the weight of the world on their shoulders. It brings me the greatest joy to see girls play with dolls, play outside, jump, get messy, and chase each other. I love seeing the boys outside playing volleyball with the girls or playing basketball together. They get to enjoy being a child, and that is a gift to them and joy to all of us who work in Nana's House.

Since we mainly had ladies taking care of the boys, I saw that things were stressful and there was a lack of male influence. I prayed God would send a man to cover the boys' home.

The boys needed a man in their lives. Too many had never known what it felt like to toss a ball with a dad, to hear the words "I'm proud of you," or to be taught how to stand tall in a world determined to knock them down. They needed to know they are valuable, both to us and to God. I wanted them to have a childhood that included that kind of presence—a man who would laugh with them, listen to them, and show them what it meant to grow into a good man.

In our local jail, we've been given a space where we hold weekly church services. One of the men who found faith in Jesus through our church was a wonderful person named Hugo. He was released early for good behavior, and God radically transformed his life. After his release, he began attending church, and we eventually hired him to help clean the building.

After getting to know Hugo for a couple of years, it was clear to me that God's hand was on him. I talked to several of the pastors and leaders about asking him to join our team, and everybody was in agreement. So one day I asked him, "Would you ever be interested in working with the boys' home?"

Without hesitation, he said yes.

Hugo turned out to have precisely the instincts and discernment I was hoping for. He could see things in the boys' behavior that I'd never have recognized. He's still with us today, and he and his wife now run the boys' home together. Hugo has a clear calling on his life to work with boys who have suffered abuse. He also has the instincts to know when a boy is going sideways or unable to grasp the vision of Nana's House.

God is a God of transformation; He makes all things new.

Honestly, I couldn't have asked for a better answer to my prayers. Hugo has done a great job with the boys.

I love the community that Nana's House has become—a place where hope grows even in the darkest circumstances. Even in what feels like a prison of pain or past mistakes, God is weaving a story of redemption. I have always had a dream: to see people restored, no matter what they have done. God is a God of transformation; He makes all things new. I feel privileged to be part of something that doesn't rush to judge, but instead believes in new life, second chances, and the beauty of a soul made whole.

Years later, we witnessed another radical transformation in a family separated from one another. Antonio came to us at just thirteen years old. I asked him what had happened with his mother and why CPS had sent him to Nana's House. He stared at the floor for a long moment and finally said all he knew was that one day, a truck pulled up to his house and took his mother away.

Despite his painful past, he thrived at Nana's House. He gave his heart to the Lord and even learned to play the piano so that he could help lead worship in one of our nearby small mission churches.

After a couple of years, we received news from CPS: Antonio would be leaving Nana's House. We were shocked to learn that his mother had been in prison and had recently been released. When she got out of jail, she had gone directly to CPS to get help getting her son back. CPS scheduled several meetings with the mother and son before they were reunited. She spent time in therapy and completed all the requirements CPS gave her. She got a job and rented a house, and in time, Antonio was reunited with his mother.

But the story doesn't end there. One Sunday, his mother showed up at church. To my great surprise, she had gone to our church in prison and received the Lord. She knew the pastors who run the prison ministry and are on staff with us. I was shocked! She eventually became a part of the congregation and began helping us in Nana's House.

One day, she shared her testimony with me. The reason she had been in jail wasn't because of a major crime. She was just a mother trying to provide for her son, and everything went terribly wrong in the end. She spent eight months behind bars and went through counseling so she could reunite with her son. She took the steps to become a better mother and did the work; she loves her son.

I came to admire this woman. She did everything right to piece her family back together. Today, she helps us at Nana's House, and both she and her son are part of our community.

Chapter 9

Two Homes Built and the Stories They Hold

In 2011, the wave of horrible violence in Tepic finally began to settle down. It seemed that when the new governor took office, things calmed considerably.

Around that time, we dreamed of buying property and building both a boys' home and a girls' home that would truly belong to us.

By chance, we invited a very well-known Christian singer, someone my son knew, to perform a concert here in Tepic. We had no idea that the governor had used one of her songs as the theme for his political campaign. That unexpected connection opened the door for us to meet with the governor and his wife.

I was excited about the prospect of building, though there was one place where I did not want to build: a neighborhood called Canteras.

During our meeting with the governor, my husband mentioned a low-income area of Tepic where our church had been working to help people and where we had planted a church. The governor was pleased to hear about our involvement and offered to help in any way he could. Without hesitation, my husband boldly blurted out that we wanted land to build an orphanage.

After a long process of navigating various levels of government, they donated land in Canteras.

Ironically, it turned out to be the perfect place for us to build. We started with the girls' home, though it was a slow and painstaking process.

My whole life has been a dance between making my plans and letting God lead my steps. I don't always get what I want, but I've learned that when I finally loosen my grip and trust God—even when it feels terrifying—things somehow turn out for good, often in ways I never expected.

One reason I didn't worry too much about the building project itself was that I knew my husband would take the lead. I've watched him work and build. I knew in my heart that if he started building, that house would stand.

We've survived all these years because of the beautiful generosity of people who have shared pieces of themselves with us. And thanks to them, we began building, and God began providing. It started slowly—just a little at a time—but we put every donation straight to use. And every time we thought we might run out, someone else would show up to lend a hand. Visitors came with tools in hand and hearts ready to serve.

My husband has always loved to build, and he poured his whole heart into this project—raising funds, swinging hammers, managing teams, and believing with us that this place would one day stand as a testimony of God's faithfulness. He, along with Pastor Luis Lozano, a team of pastors from La Fuente, and the construction workers we hired, spent endless hours building Nana's House.

Brick by brick, board by board, prayer by prayer, God did this.

When people come to visit, I want them to understand that what they see here isn't just a beautiful property with two lovely homes—it's a miracle. Brick by brick, board by board, prayer by prayer, God did this. And He did it through us, through our friends, and through the pastors who gave their time, sweat, and strength to make it happen.

I sincerely believe that we are called to live generously—with our time, our resources, and our hearts—so that Jesus can take what little we bring and multiply it into something eternal, just like the five loaves and two fish. Compassion moved Him then, and it still does. He doesn't send people away empty. And I believe with all my heart, He didn't bring us this far to do anything less than a miracle.

After building the houses, it felt like a dream had come true. It took two years after we moved into the girls' home to finish the boys' home. Having everyone together on the same property was wonderful. It made life so much easier for me and the other leaders because we could see all the kids every day, check in on them, laugh with them, and just be part of their lives in a real, daily way.

One of the things I love most is that we have our little school right here on the property. Many of the children who come to us have missed out on years of education, and it's heartbreaking to see how far behind they can be. But our school has become a place of hope. It's not only for the children living in Nana's House—even some of our staff members have enrolled their own children. God has given us incredible teachers who pour their hearts into these kids. Our big dream is to open a larger school right in front of Nana's House, so even more children can have the chance to learn and grow.

The neighborhood where we built Nana's House is full of need. At first, I didn't want to be in that area, but now I see how God placed us here for a reason. We have the opportunity to be a light in this community, and that fills me with immense hope and excitement. We want to help people in this neighborhood build better lives, acquire work skills, and become part of a loving Christian community where they can attend church and discover how deeply God loves them.

Through our church, we also have a ministry called *Por Amor* (For Love). It's a beautiful program that distributes clothes and reaches out to various locations around Tepic, with a primary focus in Canteras, near Nana's House. We also have another program that provides meals to children and assists them with their homework.

Our Nana's House children can participate in these two programs. Learning to give back is an essential part of life. Many of our teens help in our mission churches and enjoy serving. They learn to recognize others' needs and develop compassion.

As our homes grew, we were able to welcome even more children. Around this time, we began focusing more on teens. Many of the younger girls and boys who'd arrived at Nana's House years earlier were now teenagers themselves. The truth is, very few people want to take in teens—it seems too hard, too complicated. But for me, it's an age group I enjoy. Before long, our homes were overflowing with teenagers, each with their own stories, struggles, and potential.

Before long, our homes were overflowing with teenagers, each with their own stories, struggles, and potential.

Right in the middle of this teenage boom, a little seven-year-old boy came into our lives—Juanito. He was so different from the others we were taking in at the time. Juanito had significant developmental delays and serious problems with his legs and feet. He always walked on his tiptoes, and sometimes his feet seemed almost twisted backward, as though attached in reverse.

Despite his small frame, Juanito carried a storm inside him. He was wild, unpredictable, and impossible to ignore. One moment, he'd charm you completely, melting your heart with a shy grin or a flash of sweetness. Next, he'd erupt like a volcano, unleashing a torrent of curse words and razor-sharp insults that somehow landed with unsettling accuracy. He was tiny for his age, yet when his anger rose, it felt like a giant had stepped into the room.

And still—always—there was something lovable about him. A spark of innocence. A flicker of vulnerability that made you want to fight for him, no matter how hard it might be. We knew taking him in would be both temporary and challenging, but there was never a question that he needed someone in his corner.

Help for Juanito's feet came unexpectedly, through an entirely different crisis. One day, my husband, Dwight, was working with a saw when it slipped, slicing his finger badly. We rushed to the doctor, and while the doctor stitched him up, Dwight began talking about Juanito and his twisted feet. The doctor suggested we get X-rays immediately.

The next day, I took Juanito in for an X-ray, then returned to show the films to the doctor. He believed surgery could help and promised to connect us with Shriners Hospital, a facility specializing in complex cases like Juanito's. My heart leapt at the thought of giving this little boy a better future.

But then—just as quickly—the doctor vanished. Calls went unanswered. Messages were ignored. His assistant gave me vague excuses and polite brush-offs. It felt like watching a lifeboat drift away while we stood stranded on the shore.

Still, we didn't give up. We reached out to a doctor in Mexico City who had ties to Shriners. I sent him Juanito's X-rays, and for days I checked my phone like a nervous parent waiting for news. Finally, a message came—we had an appointment.

That's when Sonia, one of our outstanding team members, stepped up to take Juanito for his surgeries. We never sent her alone; traveling with Juanito was like traveling with a live wire. His outbursts could be explosive, sudden, and public. He cussed out nurses, doctors, and even a lady at the airport. People stared and whispered. More than once, Sonia came back with that look in her eyes that told me she had fought battles no one saw.

Juanito's parents were related by blood and addicted to drugs, and they carried the same disability he had. We believe he'd also suffered a significant head injury, which explained the sharp edge to his temper and the suddenness of his rages. None of that made the stares any easier when he was screaming in the middle of a crowded terminal.

Those trips were long. They were draining. And more than once, we wondered whether we could complete the entire process without being thrown off a plane or escorted out of a clinic. But Sonia kept showing up, and so did we.

Finally, Juanito had his first surgery. Sonia took him to Mexico City five times before he had an important surgery that significantly improved his feet. When he stood afterward, wobbly but grinning, it felt like we were watching a little boy step into a new life. He still needs more procedures, but he walks with a bit more confidence now. And that, after everything, is worth every mile, every sleepless night, and every sideways glare from strangers.

Juanito was with us for four years. He was one of the most difficult—and yet one of the most endearing—children we've ever had.

There is an organization in Guadalajara that specializes in caring for kids with special needs. They have a beautiful facility with physical therapy, doctors, dentists—everything Juanito requires. We had him for four years, and it was a very challenging case because he could be violent, but we were sad when he left.

Stories like Juanito's remind me that love often comes wrapped in challenges, and sometimes the path to help someone is anything but straightforward. But when I think of his smile and the hope in his eyes, I know every struggle was worth it.

I am so proud of our team at Nana's House. With a boy like Juanito, it would have been so easy to lose patience or let frustration take over. But instead, we met his storms with the kind of grace only God can give. He was never mistreated; he was never made to feel unwanted. Even in his worst moments, we treated him with dignity and love.

When I think of Juanito, I can't help but remember the story of the father who brought his tormented son to Jesus in Mark 9:22–25. That father had lived in a constant state of desperation, watching his child seized, thrown to the ground, and harmed by something he couldn't control or fix. He had tried everything. Even the disciples couldn't help. But when Jesus arrived, the father's plea came spilling out, raw and broken: "If You can do anything, take pity on us and help us."

I imagine the ache in his voice, the mixture of hope and exhaustion. I've heard that tone before—it's the sound of a parent or caregiver who has fought every battle and is still losing. Jesus' reply still moves me: "Everything is possible for one who believes."

And then came one of the most honest prayers in Scripture: "I do believe—help me overcome my unbelief!"

That prayer could have been mine for Juanito. He was unpredictable, explosive, and sometimes so hard to handle that it felt like we were holding on by a thread. But like that father, I knew the answer wasn't to give up—it was to bring him into the presence of Jesus, whether through prayer, patience, or simply by refusing to stop loving him.

In the Gospel story, Jesus speaks directly to the spirit tormenting the boy: "Come out of him and never enter him again!"

And in an instant, the boy was free—so free that Jesus could take his hand, lift him, and return him whole to his father.

I'm not sure if Juanito will ever experience that kind of instant deliverance. But I do know this: Every mile traveled for his surgery, every moment of patience shown in his worst outbursts, and every prayer whispered over him is part of the same hope. That one day, he will stand completely free, walking into the life God created for him. That is my hope for Juanito.

Chapter 10

Compassion Is Not a Sign of Weakness

Compassion has always been my gift, but I have not always handled it well. God has shaped it and taught me to let it flow from Him. Left to my own instincts, my compassion can spiral or go off course—but when it comes from Him, it carries wisdom.

I think compassion gets refined over time. At first, we feel sorry for people and want to help, but as we go through our own pain and struggles, something changes. Our compassion gets deeper. It's no longer just about feeling bad for someone—it's about really understanding them. I think God uses hard things in our lives to shape our hearts, to make our compassion more real and, most importantly, steady.

Here is the story of Cindy. Stories like hers matter because they reveal the very heart of what we do.

Cindy came to Nana's House at just fourteen, yet she had already endured a terrible life at the hands of her mother and stepfather. People exploited her and forced her to grow up far too soon. Her past included several lost pregnancies, brought about by abuse no child should ever experience. Her stepfather's abuse was extreme, including making films of his stepdaughter. We were not told any of this before she came to us, so we were in the dark.

Despite all she had been through, she was polite and helpful, and she carried herself with a maturity that surprised me. In the end, I realized she wanted to do everything right and to be accepted and loved.

For a while, everything seemed peaceful—until another girl arrived with a similar history. They quickly bonded, but the connection took a difficult turn, leading to dishonesty, stealing, and behaviors that revealed deep, unhealed wounds in both. Lying and stealing are things we expect at first because many of these children did both to survive, but it went deeper than that. The months that followed were a tough time at Nana's House.

We always know that when teens come to us, they've been through a lot. But one of the hardest lessons has been learning to discern which kids truly want what we're offering—a chance at healing, stability, and a new life—and which ones are determined to pull us into their own unhealthy world.

We're patient with them. We give them space and time to grow. But sometimes, their goal isn't to adjust to a healthy way of life. It's to pull us into theirs: unhealthy habits, toxic attitudes, laziness, disrespect.

God was trying to get a message through to me, but in my stubbornness, it took a long time to really hear it. I needed to learn to let go of some cases—kids who worked hard to pull others toward their own ideas of what was right, even when those ideas went directly against everything we stood for. Some of them tried to recruit others into things that were harmful and unsafe.

Even when I knew it was time to let go, I struggled to do it—until I ended up in handcuffs.

We wanted every child who came to truly understand what we were offering and to see the heart behind what we were doing. But that wasn't always the case, and even when I knew it was time to let go, I struggled to do it—until I ended up in handcuffs.

That is the day I got a clue. I did not just need to redefine my compassion—it required a complete makeover.

At that time, we were receiving many teens, but no one was sending us their backgrounds or profiles. We had to rely on our own interviews, and that's where my naïve compassion showed. I listened with my heart but didn't yet have the wisdom to see the story behind the story. A perfect storm was forming, and though I sensed something wasn't right, I couldn't name it.

The truth was hard to grasp. Some had fallen into addiction, and others had been sold into prostitution by their own families. They had grown up surrounded by lies, betrayal, and crime. I couldn't discern the depth of it all because I was stepping into a world of brokenness I had never known.

God began refining not only my compassionate heart, but the staff's as well. I learned that genuine compassion doesn't mean ignoring the truth. It means seeing it clearly and still choosing to love.

But love also protects. For the sake of the other children, the staff, and even myself, there had to be limits. Some cases were simply too severe for us to handle, so we placed those children in facilities equipped to care for them.

As I've said, the authorities didn't give me the complete information back then, and learning that lesson was complicated and costly. Now, if Child Protective Services doesn't provide full details about a child's background, we simply say no. It's not a lack of compassion—it's wisdom, refined by experience and guided by God.

In the midst of learning a life lesson, a lot of good things were happening. One example is Regina. CPS took Regina away from the only home she'd ever known—a small village that had raised her after her mother walked out one day and never returned. From then on, they passed her from house to house, vulnerable to people who wanted to take advantage of her.

When she first came to Nana's House, she cried for over six hours straight, sobbing that she just wanted to go home. She was such a sweet, gentle girl that my heart broke at the thought of losing her. I told her we'd talk to the authorities to see if there was any way she could return to her village.

But the very next day, she surprised me. She wiped her tears, looked me in the eyes, and said she'd decided to stay. Now, she is going to high school, and she is working in our coffee shop. She is so helpful that she has been mistaken for staff when authorities come to Nana's House. She is still with us, and she's family now.

Another is Maria, a teenage girl who had been accused of killing her aunt and using drugs. When she walked through our doors, she was pale and exhausted, with dark circles under her eyes and a sadness that weighed on her like a heavy coat. Her family insisted she'd killed her aunt because she'd misbehaved that day and caused her aunt to die. But none of it was true.

And in time, we discovered the truth of who she really was: one of the sweetest souls we've ever had the privilege to know.

And then there's the young teen boy whose own mother tried to kill him. He's endured unthinkable trauma, and he still struggles. But he's trying. He's learning. He's getting involved in church, discovering new things, and slowly building a sense of hope.

Every child who comes to us writes a story of resilience, courage, and unexpected new beginnings.

Many teens have chosen to stay, living out the experience of having a home and being surrounded by people who believe in them.

At Nana's House, we're not just a shelter. We are a place where children can feel at home while they are here. And every child who comes to us writes a story of resilience, courage, and unexpected new beginnings.

Over the years, we've welcomed several boys into Nana's House who arrived bruised and broken. Often, if a boy is sent to us beaten up by his dad, it's because the boy has declared he is gay, and what followed was not grace or even confusion, but rage and violence.

I am aware that this is a sensitive and often contentious topic, particularly within Christian communities. My advice to these families is: Please let the family know violence is not the proper reaction and never will be. Talk to your child; pray for your child. They just shared something challenging for them to share. I believe you can disagree with someone and still love them.

Our response to these young men is one of gentleness and kindness, and that has left an impact far greater than we could have imagined. We don't have all the answers, but we know that God's love heals. And while they're with us, we have the beautiful opportunity to show them a different side of faith—a side that reflects the real heart of God.

One young man stays vivid in my memory. He showed up at Nana's House full of life, a big personality that instantly filled the room. He'd recently come out as gay to his family, and the fallout was explosive.

In his fear and frustration, he hadn't handled things well. The conflict escalated into physical violence—violence he had initiated. That's why they removed him from his home, sent him to juvenile hall, and then to us. He was deeply ashamed of his actions and carried a heavy sadness over the hurt he'd caused. But even in the middle of all that turmoil, I could see the goodness in him. A light still shone in his eyes —something genuine that nothing had managed to extinguish.

We spent hours talking. He was funny, open-hearted, and honest, and it wasn't long before he'd charmed the entire staff. He began attending church with us and, over time, decided to become a Christian. He brought his whole family to church; he is faithful and an active part of our church community. I love his story because he truly saw and understood the love of God.

Though he no longer lives at Nana's House, he still comes back often—sometimes just to hang out, other times to join us on special outings. In many ways, he has become part of our Nana's House family, a living reminder that family isn't just about who shares your roof, but also about who welcomes you, believes in you, and loves you right where you are.

Jesus often surprised people by whom He chose to spend time. He didn't stick to the "acceptable" crowd or those who looked the part of a righteous person. Instead, He went to the places no one expected, sat with the outcasts, and spoke to those everyone else overlooked. He befriended tax collectors, healed the sick, and welcomed sinners—people who didn't fit the rules of respectability. His love wasn't selective; it didn't wait for people to be "good enough." That's what confused everyone who thought they understood God. Jesus showed that the heart of God reaches beyond appearances, beyond labels, and beyond our human judgments.

I want to be like that. So, if you see me hanging around the "wrong" people, you can be assured I'm sharing the heart of Jesus. Even though I know my compassion could sometimes go wrong, God has tamed me to use His wisdom. But sometimes I feel like people are quick to judge. They misinterpret the way we react as "liberal." God gave me a heart that cares deeply. His love and understanding usually hit the mark where it matters most. I want my heart to learn from that, to love like He does, even when it's complicated or confusing.

Compassion is never a sign of weakness. True compassion is born of strength—it takes courage to care, to stand with the hurting, and to love when it's hard. Strength and compassion are not opposites; they are inseparable.

Chapter 11

The Storm

As I mentioned before, the large group of teens we had on the new property was a volatile mix. Some truly wanted to change, while others carried their own hidden agendas. The atmosphere felt uneasy, like the calm before the storm. My staff and I could sense something was off, but none of us could have imagined just how bad it was about to get.

I really believed that these teens would eventually want a positive change in their lives, but I was wrong.

We were hosting a team that came to help us in Nana's House. They were a church group from the United States. One peaceful, sunny day, while the team was planting flowers and a tree, I got an urgent call from a young woman who had grown up in Nana's House.

All she said was that three girls from Nana's House were being detained for shoplifting, and that the police were being called to arrest them.

At first, I thought, *Okay, I'll just go and explain we work with Child Protective Services and ask them to please understand that the police would need to wait for CPS to arrive.*

I didn't even flinch. Not at first. No big deal, I told myself. I'd walk in, explain who we were, assure the store's management that sometimes kids arrive with rough edges from their past, offer to pay for whatever the girls took, and leave. That was the script in my head.

But when I arrived, the script dissolved. The manager's eyes were icy; his expression carved from stone. He looked at me like I was a criminal. He said, "These girls are going to jail."

The words slammed into me. "Please," I begged, "We work with CPS. Wait for them to arrive and handle the situation." But my pleas slid right off their hardened faces.

And then the police arrived. The atmosphere shifted from uncomfortable to scary. The managers pointed fingers at me, their accusation venomous: I had taught the girls to steal. My chest burned. I opened my mouth to defend myself—only to be cut down.

"Shut up!" one officer barked, his voice sharp and commanding. It wasn't just a warning. It was a threat.

My heart lurched. Something was wrong—terribly wrong. These men weren't neutral; they weren't listening, nor were they protecting. They were after me.

I thought about all the times I'd walked through this store, exchanging smiles with the staff. I thought they knew me. I thought they liked me. But standing there under the weight of their stares, I realized I had been wrong. In their eyes, I wasn't a protector of children. I wasn't a neighbor. I was an outsider. Suspicious. Dangerous.

My heart lurched. Something was wrong— terribly wrong.

I tried to explain, desperate now, listing the names of authorities we worked with in CPS, hoping it would validate me. But the harder I tried, the colder their eyes became. They thought I was bluffing, pulling rank, playing a game. My words weren't landing—they were detonating.

Over thirty-five years of living in Mexico, I had always been treated with dignity by the police. Respect. Even kindness. But this was different.

My daughter, Rebecca, rushed in, protective and ready to stand by my side. But the hostility swallowed her too. Shouts. Hands grabbing. And then—the cold bite of handcuffs. My daughter and I were shoved like criminals into a police truck, metal clanging, wrists burning, faces exposed to a gawking crowd.

Many of our pastors showed up, trying to help, to no avail. Dwight, my husband, was out of town, so he couldn't help me. I felt bad that he had to hear about all this without having any way to assist us.

Sirens. Doors slamming. Police cars multiplying around us like vultures circling prey. Over what? Nail polish. Candy. Three terrified girls who barely understood what was happening.

Humiliation crashed over me. Being arrested was a line I never thought I'd cross—a moment I could not unlive.

They dragged us into the police station, wrists cinched in handcuffs, and shoved us into hard plastic chairs. Then they left us to wait. One hour. Then two. Then three. By the fourth, my body throbbed with pain, and my mind spun with dread. This time wasn't a small storm—it was one raging beyond control.

Everyone knew the rule in our town: If the police arrested you on a Friday, you were going to jail for the weekend. No exceptions. The thought pounded in my head like a relentless drumbeat. Friday meant two nights behind bars.

Rebecca sat beside me. The girls were somewhere else.

My son came. My lawyer tried. But the officers slammed the door shut on both. "No one talks to them." They cut us off, silenced.

I whispered prayers under my breath. *Lord, please— send someone. Anyone. Help us.* The words rose like smoke in a suffocating room.

Then the air shifted. Boots pounded against the tile floor. A figure approached. An officer dressed head to toe in black, helmet gleaming, weapons strapped across his chest.

My stomach tightened. Was this it? Were they moving us deeper inside? But then, he pulled off his helmet. His eyes were wet with tears.

Rebecca gasped. "José! We are so happy to see you. Please, help us!"

It was like seeing a lifeline appear in the storm. José wasn't just a police officer—he was one of our friends. He had sat in our church, worshipped with us. And now, here he was, standing between us and disaster.

He moved fast, straight to the head officer. Words flew. Authority clashed. And then—click. The handcuffs were off. My wrists burned with relief. The storm was calming down.

They ushered us into the chief's office, tension in the air. The chief watched the store's security footage in silence, scanning every frame. Then he looked up, eyes narrowed, studying me like he was trying to read the truth on my face.

"*Señora*," he said slowly, "I have never seen anyone fight so passionately for children in need. I'm impressed."

The weight began to lift. José stayed close, making sure we got home safely. The storm that had threatened to break us finally started to calm.

But later, the second storm began to rage. The truth was that almost every one of my girls had stolen from that store. That day was more than just an arrest. It was a shattering—a wake-up call.

Everything snapped into focus. I'd been walking through that store feeling like a hero, convinced I was doing the right thing. But to management, I wasn't a hero at all. I was the villain they were waiting to catch. The girls had lit the fuse, and I stepped right onto the bomb. When it went off, everything I thought I understood about that moment blew apart. First came the fury, then the heartbreak—and in the end, a kind of wisdom I could never have gained any other way.

First came the fury, then the heartbreak—and in the end, a kind of wisdom I could never have gained any other way.

Beautiful Chaos

For months, we stretched ourselves thin, facing increasingly volatile behavior from the teens placed in our care. Later, we learned the truth—the authorities never should have sent many of those girls and boys to Nana's House. They needed a place with structured interventions far beyond what a family-style home like ours could provide. We had taken them in anyway, believing we could help, thinking love and the structure we had in place were enough. And sometimes it was—but not always.

That day, everything came to a head. The dream I had started Nana's House with—warmth, safety, family—collided with a brutal reality I could no longer ignore.

I could have dug in and demanded we keep doing things the old way, clinging to the vision that once worked. But sitting in that truck, handcuffed along with my daughter, I knew something had to change.

So, I prayed. I was ready and willing to hear God and change things. I realized that it was time to strip everything down. Time to ask God what He wanted Nana's House to become. Time to face the truth, no matter what that meant. It was time to reevaluate everything.

We've since restructured our approach—not to be controlling, but to maintain the peace of the home.

Today, only high school students are allowed to have phones, and even then, they must turn them in at night or after school. We check content when necessary. Younger children don't have access to phones or the internet, except in supervised educational settings.

Upstairs access is restricted. No children are allowed to go up there in groups without permission; we need to see what they are doing. Music is welcome, but anything that glorifies violence or contains explicit content is banned. We carefully approve all movies and shows.

Video games? We don't allow them. Our kids have experienced too much trauma to play most video games. It triggers all kinds of things for our kids in Nana's House.

When a situation is beyond us, we don't pretend we can handle it. We act fast. We either call for help or ensure the child is placed in a setting where they can receive the specialized care they need.

These boundaries have brought peace back to Nana's House. I still believe in the heart of what we started, but I've learned that even the best ideas must bend when reality demands it. I didn't hold onto the past just because it worked before. I let God and our team lead us into a new season of wisdom and stability.

After walking through the gut-wrenching experience of being arrested and seeing it splashed across the local newspaper, I came to a difficult but necessary realization: It wasn't just the structure of Nana's House that needed changing—it was me, too.

For years, I had filled my life and home with children and teenagers. I gave everything I had to the ministry I believed God had called me to. And to be honest, I am proud of what my team and I built. We loved those kids fiercely. We created a place where they were safe, where they could laugh, where they could be kids again.

But somewhere along the way, I forgot that my house was also my home. And more importantly, it was our home—mine and my incredibly patient husband's. A man who never once complained about kids occupying his space, taking over our kitchen table, our living room, or our privacy. I had let the ministry creep into every inch of our lives, and while my heart was in the right place, my boundaries were not.

So I made a decision—I took my home back. Not because I was done with the kids or the calling, but because I finally realized how much of myself I had lost in the process. I needed to enjoy my own space again. I needed to sit with my husband in peace. I needed to breathe.

More than anything, I needed to admit something that had been tugging at my soul for a long time: I was trying to be the savior. I wanted so badly to show every child what love could look like and what a healthy home could feel like. But some of these children came to us so broken, so traumatized, that what they needed the most was for God to touch their hearts and heal the damage. The truth is, God never meant for me to have the cure.

Only God can heal a soul. Only He can transform the heart.

And part of my healing journey was learning to say, "God, I'm tired. I'm overwhelmed. I've done what I can. Now, You take the reins." I had to learn to be human again. To be okay with not having all the answers. To trust that God never asked me to carry it all.

Only God can heal a soul. Only He can transform the heart.

Jesus said in Matthew 11:28–30, "Come to me, all you who are weary and burdened, and I will give you rest… for my yoke is easy and my burden is light."

And 1 Corinthians 3:6–7 reminded me: "I planted the seed, Apollos watered it, but God has been making it grow… only God… makes things grow."

And only God makes things heal, I realized. I had taken on too much emotionally. I had made myself responsible for every outcome, every heartbreak, every child that walked away from Nana's House flipping me off or—God help me—getting me arrested. That hurt. Deeply. But then I thought about Jesus. Ten lepers healed. Only one came back to say thank you.

The moment I truly let go, everything shifted. I still work. I still care. But now I do it with open hands. I say yes when the Lord leads me, not when guilt pushes me. I help others not because it defines me, but because it's what I was made for.

And in that surrender, I found peace. I traded my striving for His rest, my anxious control for His faithful sovereignty.

The truth is, Nana's House will go on. The ministry will grow. But not because I'm holding it all together. It will grow because God is faithful. He's not asking me to be Him—He's asking me to trust Him.

I'm not the Savior. I never was. I am the servant. And that, I'm learning, is more than enough.

One of the most comforting truths in Scripture is that God is a Father to the fatherless. He sees the orphan. He sees the abandoned, forgotten, or passed-over child. And not only does He see them—He steps in. "A father to the fatherless, a defender of widows, is God in his holy dwelling" (Psalm 68:5).

When the world walks away, God draws near. He doesn't just care about orphans from a distance; He identifies as their Father. That's not symbolic. It's personal. He enters into their pain and becomes the One who protects, nurtures, and provides.

God shows His heart for orphans and abandoned children through Nana's House and Heart4Mexico. We are His hands—offering hugs, providing meals, creating family. He uses us to reflect His love, but ultimately, as the children grow, they need to see that it's God Himself who brings true healing.

He's the One who called us, not just to meet needs, but to reveal His heart. These children matter deeply to Him. And through our obedience, they begin to discover that truth for themselves.

One of my favorite verses is Psalm 27:10, "Though my father and mother forsake me, the Lord will receive me." This verse is powerful for any child who has felt rejected by the very people who should have protected them most. Earthly parents may fail, but God does not. He steps into that space of loss and becomes the stable, unshakable presence they need. If a person does not recognize the need for God to step in and realize that only God can truly heal, they will sadly continue to feel abandoned.

Another verse I love is Psalm 82:3. "Defend the weak and the fatherless; uphold the cause of the poor and the oppressed." As His people, God calls us to mirror His heart. That's why we do what we do at Nana's House. We step in—not to be saviors, but to reflect the heart of the One who is. We don't pretend to have all the answers, but we know the One who does. And He promises not to leave His children alone.

Chapter 12
Their Stories Matter

As many complaints as I have about CPS in Mexico, I must admit that the benefits outweigh the criticisms.

Now, when it comes to CPS, one thing I do appreciate is the accountability. They keep a close eye on us. We have an open-door policy with them—even if sometimes I wish the door had a peephole and a delay button.

At first, their surprise inspections upset me. Now I just treat them like uninvited relatives popping in for dinner. You straighten your shirt, smile big, and hope nobody is screaming in the background.

One day, I was working at the girls' home when Mateo had an epic meltdown. He could be belligerent even on a good day—and this was not a good day. We had already requested CPS's help with him, to no avail.

That day, I gave up trying to reason with him and told the other kids, "Just ignore him. Let him throw what he wants. He'll calm down eventually, and when he does, he'll be the one cleaning up the mess."

Sure enough, he started tossing puzzle pieces, papers, and anything else he could get his hands on, hoping to get a reaction. I watched from the corner of my eye, refusing to take the bait. He was getting increasingly frustrated because I wouldn't scold him, yell, or wrestle the puzzle box out of his hands, even though he clearly wanted me to.

Then the doorbell rang.

I crossed the little pathway to open the door, praying it was someone who didn't care about appearances. Nope. It was a line of CPS officers. *Eight* of them. The lead one smiled and said, "We're here for a surprise inspection. We'll be interviewing all the children separately, without staff present."

I froze. Behind me, in full view, was Mateo—grinning like he just won the lottery and flipping me off with both hands through the office window.

I didn't know how to react. I think I did a mix of all three internally. The house was a disaster, Mateo was in the middle of a rampage, and CPS was getting a front-row seat. I had asked for help with this child, and they hadn't lifted a finger. But now? Oh, now they show up.

Then I thought, *Oh well.* I looked at the lady in charge and said, "Have fun. And by the way, the first thing you guys need to do is get Mateo to stop flipping us all off and get him out of the office."

And you know what happened next? Mateo—yes, the same kid who was just flipping me off—suddenly transformed into the most polite, charming little host you've ever seen. The CPS ladies were absolutely gushing over him. "What a sweet boy!" they said, thoroughly impressed.

All I could do was smile, nod, and think, *Oh well.*

Moments like this remind me that the messiness of serving and loving people is at the heart of the gospel. Consider Jesus on the cross. The cross was not just a moment in history—it was the loudest "I love you" ever spoken to a broken world. "Greater love has no one than this: to lay down one's life for one's friends" (John 15:13).

Jesus didn't die because He was overpowered. He died because He was willing. Willing to step into the brokenness of our lives, into the mess, the pain, the hopelessness—and bring healing not with formulas, but with Himself.

To me, that is the definition of Beautiful Chaos. It's the mess of humanity met with the grace of a Savior. And at Nana's House, I see glimpses of that every day.

People often look at what we're doing and say, "I want to do that too." And I say—that's beautiful, if you're willing to live among the brokenness. If you're willing to sit with pain that doesn't always resolve, to love people who may never express gratitude, and to keep showing up when your ideas, plans, and best efforts fall short.

There's no magic formula to put broken hearts back together. Sometimes it takes years before you see even a sliver of progress. Sometimes, you never see it at all. And yet, we keep going. Not because we're heroes, but because Jesus already did the hard part. He died for all of us, so we don't need to hang on a cross—we just need to be there for people. To offer what little we have, mixed with the limitless love of God.

You need the kind of grace that can absorb the chaos without being destroyed by it.

But here's the hard truth: If you're going to step into the world of orphan care, foster care, or deep, messy ministry, you must come armed with grace, not just good intentions. You need the kind of grace that can absorb the chaos without being destroyed by it. Because I've seen people try to do this in their own strength—and I've watched them break. They lose sleep. They lose peace. Some even lose themselves.

Maybe you're thinking, *How hard could it be?* Let me lovingly say: Stop right there. This work is not for the faint of heart. But if you're ready to walk into the messiness, trusting that God's love can still bring beauty out of it—then welcome. You're in the right place.

Beautiful chaos isn't about perfection. It's about presence. It's about showing up with empty hands and a willing heart. And letting the grace of God do what only He can do.

We once took in two young indigenous girls who arrived at Nana's House in heartbreaking condition. They were timid and quiet, their clothes barely hanging on them—ripped skirts stained from wear, their hair matted and crawling with lice. Their eyes, though gentle, seemed distant, almost clouded by something we couldn't yet understand.

The CPS worker who brought them told us, rather casually, that the girls had "a small issue with their sight." That was a massive understatement. Within the first hour, it became evident that one of the sisters was completely blind, and the other could only see in blurs and shadows. We were shocked. Nothing had prepared us for this. I wasn't trained to care for blind children, and our staff—though full of heart—lacked the tools and knowledge to support their needs appropriately.

I called CPS right away and said, "You told me she had a slight vision issue, but she's completely blind. We don't have the tools or training to help someone who's blind. We're going to need help."

They assured me they had a better placement for them, but "details still needed to be worked out." So, the girls stayed.

In the meantime, I wasn't going to sit around waiting. I took both girls to a specialist, praying—honestly pleading—that there might be some treatment or surgery that could help. I hoped maybe the girl who had limited sight could have it corrected or improved, and deep in my heart, I even dared to hope there was a miracle out there for the one who was entirely blind.

The doctor was kind but direct. After examining them, he explained that their indigenous tribe had a known genetic condition that caused progressive blindness in many of its children. "There is no cure," he said gently. "This is irreversible."

It hit me like a wave of grief. I wasn't just sad for the girls—I was angry at how easily they dismissed their situation. How many others were out there, silently suffering, mislabeled as having a "slight problem"? How often are children's fundamental needs minimized because they don't fit neatly into a system?

Despite the challenges, those few months with the girls became an unexpectedly beautiful chapter in our story.

We had new skirts made for them in the bright colors of their tribal heritage—each thread a tiny act of dignity and restoration. I watched them slowly come to life. They laughed. They played, they listened to music, and although they couldn't see, they could feel. They sat with the other girls at meals and found comfort in our routine. We even taught the other children how to gently guide and include them in play, which created a kind of tenderness in the home we hadn't seen before.

When the time finally came for them to transition to the home they would be living in, we didn't just wave goodbye. We sent them off with love and gifts: two beds, bedding, clothes, food, toys, everything we could gather. It was as if the whole house came together to say, "You matter."

That experience changed us. It reminded us that love doesn't always look like fixing something. Sometimes it seems like just showing up, listening, adjusting, and doing your best with what you have. It's not about being the hero—it's about creating a moment of dignity in a life that's seen too little of it.

Love doesn't always look like fixing something.

Those girls taught us something precious: You don't have to see the world clearly to feel loved in it. For a few sacred months, they knew what it meant to be deeply loved.

Here in Tepic, there are two indigenous tribes that are part of the soul of our community. The Cora and Huichol peoples each carry their own languages, faiths, traditions, and cultural beauty. You can feel it in the rhythm of their speech, the colors of their art, and the strength of their resilience.

But not everyone sees it that way. Though the world praises these cultures in museums and tourist brochures, many still look down on them. That's why at Nana's House, I'm quick to correct any child who uses "Cora" or "Huichol" as an insult. We teach our children to respect the deep heritage of these people. The Huichol are globally known for their exquisite beadwork and intricate yarn paintings. The Cora, with their calm dignity and lyrical language, carry a rich legacy of tradition and strength. Many from these tribes have gone on to achieve the highest levels of education, despite the prejudice they've faced.

I remember walking into the British Museum for the first time and being stopped in my tracks by a towering display of Huichol art. It was radiant, holding its place with dignity in one of the world's most prestigious spaces. And I thought, *If only every child from these tribes could see this, they could know how priceless their culture truly is.*

One child who reminded me of that value was José, a four-year-old boy who came to us completely silent. Not a word. We wondered if he was too traumatized to speak. But then I realized: this little one didn't speak Spanish. He spoke Cora.

His silence wasn't fear—it was language—a language we didn't understand.

Slowly, he began to learn Spanish, picking it up bit by bit. Even then, he remained reserved, always observing, always listening. There was a soft strength in him, the kind that doesn't demand attention but stays with you long after the room has emptied.

Around that time, I knew of a missionary couple who had longed to adopt. José—as we called him—was waiting. They started the long, sometimes exhausting adoption process with grace and patience. And in time, everything fell into place.

Today, that same little boy who once spoke only Cora now speaks fluent Spanish and English. He's thriving in a loving family—one of the sweetest I've ever met. Seeing him now, full of life and voice and confidence, is one of those full-circle moments that fills your heart to the brim. This story began in silence and misunderstanding, but it ended in connection, language, family, and love.

Over the years, we've welcomed many indigenous children into Nana's House, each one carrying a story that deserves to be honored. And we will keep opening our doors, our hearts, and our ears—not just to the children, but to their cultures, their voices, and the incredible richness they bring to our world.

I love the story of the blind beggar and Jesus letting everybody know he mattered, found in Mark 10:46–52. Bartimaeus sat by the road outside Jericho—blind, begging, and ignored. When he heard Jesus was passing by, hope rose in him. He shouted, "Jesus, Son of David, have mercy on me!"

The crowd told him to be quiet, but he cried out even louder. Rejected by people, he refused to give up.

Then Jesus stopped. "Call him," He said.

Bartimaeus threw off his cloak and came to Jesus. "What do you want me to do for you?" Jesus asked.

"Rabbi, I want to see."

"Go, your faith has healed you," Jesus said.

In an instant, sight returned. The man, once silenced, now saw the face of mercy itself. Rejected by the world, Bartimaeus was accepted—and transformed—by Jesus.

That moment speaks to me so deeply because it reflects the heart of what we believe at Nana's House and in our church community. Similar to Bartimaeus, the children who come to us are often overlooked, misunderstood, or pushed aside by the world. But not by us—and not by Jesus. We don't care where someone comes from, what language they speak, what they've been through, or what challenges they carry.

They matter.

They are seen.

They are welcome.

At Nana's House, we get to be like the people Jesus told to "call him." We get to say to hurting, overlooked children: "Come. He's calling you. You matter here."

And in our church, the same is true. Whether you come with baggage, questions, brokenness, or blindness of your own, there's a place for you. Just like Bartimaeus, you don't have to stay silent. You can call out to Jesus. And He will stop for you, too.

We took in a beautiful little girl named Lupita who had suffered a heartbreaking injury. She was sweet, gentle, and easy to care for—but her tiny leg told a different story.

We get to say to hurting, overlooked children: "Come. He's calling you. You matter here."

In a moment of anger, someone had struck her with a machete, leaving her with severe damage to her leg that required surgery.

We cared for her. Despite everything she'd been through, Lupita was sweet and easy to be around. In time, she received the surgery she desperately needed. And not long after, something even more wonderful happened—a lovely couple adopted Lupita.

Her story, which began in pain and fear, became one of healing, hope, and a new beginning.

All these stories—beautiful, messy, heartbreaking, and hope-filled—matter because the children matter. Their lives, their resilience, their dignity are the point. But alongside that, I've discovered something unexpected. As I've been allowed to walk with them, to show up in ordinary and often messy ways, I've found joy, fulfillment, and purpose.

It's easy to assume that when you step into ministry, you're the one doing the giving. But what I've found, time and time again, is that I've been on the receiving end more than I ever expected. Through these children and the people I work with, I've discovered not only purpose, but fellowship. I've been shaped, stretched, and changed in ways I never imagined.

I wasn't born in this country, often standing out with my *gringa* face and foreign accent in a town where there aren't many like me. And yet, this has become my home. These people have become my people.

Laughter over shared meals, inside jokes with coworkers, crying with someone whose pain echoes your own—those moments have become my treasure. Belonging is one of the richest gifts life can offer, and I've found it here, in unexpected places, with people who have invited me not just into their homes but into their hearts.

The joy I've found isn't from fixing others but from walking with them. If my only goal were to change people, I would never have truly entered into fellowship. I would have stood above them, not beside them. That kind of posture leaves no room for friendship. It places you on a platform instead of around the table.

Jesus sat at the table with sinners, with His disciples, and even with Judas—the one who would betray Him. Over and over in the New Testament, we see Him breaking bread with people, sharing meals that were far more than food. In that culture, the table was sacred ground. To sit with someone was to enter into fellowship, to share life, to acknowledge their worth.

The table is where masks come off. It's where we tell stories, where laughter rises, tears fall, and hearts are knit together. Jesus chose that place—not the synagogue, not the palace, not the public square—as the setting for some of His most profound moments with people. He invited the righteous and the broken, the faithful and the doubters, knowing that fellowship at the table had the power to heal, to challenge, and to transform.

When Jesus sat at the table, He wasn't just eating; He was showing us that genuine fellowship happens when we draw close, when we share, and when we allow others into our lives—even those we find hardest to love.

So no, these stories aren't just about ministry. They're about community. The kind that's messy and real, where people bump into each other's flaws but also hold each other up. They're also about healing, the kind that doesn't always come with a quick prayer or a perfect solution, but through time, presence, and love that refuses to give up. And finally, they're about joy—the kind you find in unexpected laughter around a dinner table, or in a child's smile that reminds you why you keep going when it feels too hard.

Because the truth is, God's work is never one-directional. He doesn't just use us to touch lives, to serve, or to build His kingdom. He also uses every encounter, every broken story, every shared meal, and every late-night conversation to shape us. He molds our character through the very people we think we are helping. He breaks our pride through their honesty. He teaches us resilience through their survival. And He softens our hearts by showing us His reflection in places we never thought to look.

Ultimately, ministry isn't about us swooping in to change the world. It's about learning to walk with people in a way that changes the world, making us more like Jesus, who chose to dwell among us, sit at our tables, and be changed in His humanity even as He changed eternity.

Ministry isn't about us swooping in to change the world. It's about learning to walk with people in a way that changes the world, making us more like Jesus,

God sent His own Son to live in a time of history where superstition reigned and comforts were few. Into this flawed world, Jesus came as a baby. The King of Kings chose to arrive not with power, but with weakness. He was tiny, fragile, and entirely dependent on others. He grew up in a specific culture, surrounded by customs and culture, by rituals and superstitions. Imagine the ignorance, the strange medical remedies, the fears of evil spirits, the endless rules about what made someone clean or unclean. And yet, He didn't dismiss all of it—He lived within it.

Jesus learned the language, kept the traditions, ate the food, and walked the dusty roads with ordinary people. He saw their desperation to be healed and whole. He didn't roll His eyes at their beliefs—He met them in their chaos with compassion.

After living in Mexico for so many years, I've come to realize that this is what real love looks like—not fixing from afar, but stepping into the mess, the mystery, and the beautiful chaos of someone else's world. That's what Jesus did. And that's what I want to do too.

Jesus is the greatest missionary of all time. He didn't just preach from a distance. He moved in. He made a home among broken people. He lived among them, endured their misunderstandings, and eventually laid down His life for them—for us.

And that's what wrecks me. Because here I am, years into serving in another culture, and I still catch myself wanting to escape the chaos, still tempted to cling to what I once thought was "normal." But Jesus never clung to comfort. He entered the world fully, embraced all it had to offer—the strange, the sacred, the flawed—and He did it for love.

Chapter 13

Beauty from Brokenness

Let me be honest—loving others is not always easy. I'm not some big mush ball of unconditional affection, floating through life, overlooking everyone's flaws with a serene smile on my face. No, there are days I'm irritable, weary, and stretched far too thin. Running two homes for vulnerable children is beautiful, but it's also full of challenges. The washing machines seem to be in a constant state of rebellion. The property needs upkeep—trash to haul, weeds to pull, endless cleaning. The kids act out. The staff have their off days. And I, too, have mine.

Community doesn't just magically happen because we all love Jesus. Building a place of peace and belonging takes intentional, backbreaking work. It takes grace. It takes grit. And more often than I'd like to admit, it takes pleading with God in the quiet corners of Nana's House—while folding laundry or calming a child in the middle of a rage. In those moments, I whisper prayers through clenched teeth: *Lord, help me. Change me. Make me more like You.*

There are moments when I want to retreat, to throw my hands up and say, "This is too much." But instead, I've learned to pause, breathe, and make a mental list of every small victory I can find. A child who is finally calming down and trusting us. A staff member who went the extra mile. A teen who didn't run away this week. I rehearse the good things because gratitude reorients my heart and helps me rise above the chaos.

That's when I can encourage others—not with fake cheer, but with a deep, anchored joy. I can lift the staff, speak life over the kids, and remind even my own soul that God is with us in this.

Jesus said, "Pick up your cross and follow Me" (Matthew 16:24). That's not just about suffering, it's about transformation. It's about choosing Christlikeness even when everything in you wants to quit. Taming character flaws, confronting selfishness, and walking in peace are all possible, but only when we decide that love isn't a feeling—it's a decision. One we have to make daily.

What's interesting is that many of the kids who have left still call again—sometimes weeks later, sometimes years. You can hear in their voice that they're not doing well. But they don't want to sever the connection entirely. So, I answer. I listen. I speak words of encouragement, even when I know they're heading down a road that won't lead to life. It's one of the hardest parts of this work—loving people even when they're pushing you away.

Over the years, I've poured my heart into people—time, love, sleepless nights, and more prayers than I can count. And still, some have walked away. Not quietly, not with gratitude, but storming out—angry, offended, sometimes cursing me on their way out. It doesn't make sense to me. I gave them everything I had, but sometimes what I had wasn't what they needed.

I've had to face the hard truth: Giving until you're empty is not the same as providing what heals. For a long time, I believed that if I just poured out more love, more time, more energy, maybe it would patch up the holes in someone else's soul. But it doesn't work that way. That's a flawed approach, because ultimately I can't fill another person's emptiness. None of us can.

The truth is that every human relationship has limits. We can walk with people, we can love them fiercely, we can pray until our knees are sore—but we cannot be what only God is meant to be. Sooner or later, everyone must discover that no person, no home, no mentor, and no ministry will ever be enough. That ache inside them, that longing for wholeness and meaning—it can't be satisfied by me, or by Nana's House, or by anything this world can give.

We cannot be what only God is meant to be.

It's not about me failing. It's about young people waking up to the truth that nobody—not a parent, not a pastor, not even a friend—can be all they need. Only God can. Sometimes the anger they throw at me is really disappointment that I can't do what only He can. It hurts to watch, but in the end, it's the most important lesson of all: You will never find healing, peace, and joy in another person—they're found in Him.

So, when they leave angry, I let them go with a broken heart—but also with peace. Because I know I pointed them to the One who is enough. Whether they recognize it now or years down the road, that truth will still be waiting for them.

Because we're in the capital city, we are close to the state's juvenile hall. When one of our teens who had left Nana's House the year before ended up there for several months, I visited, prayed, encouraged, and stood by him as best I could. It wasn't glamorous. It wasn't easy. But that's where love goes. To the hard places.

There was another young man who was so bright and full of potential, one of those kids you can just see making it. He did well in school and had dreams. But one day, he chose to leave Nana's House and move back in with his family. Not long after, he went out partying, got behind the wheel, and crashed a car. The accident killed him. I still carry that ache.

This kind of work is not always filled with happy endings. It's not always as joyous or rewarding as people might imagine. But I've learned to rest in one truth: We planted good seeds. Every child, every teen who has passed through our doors has heard the truth that they are loved, that they matter, that God's arms are always open, even when they've run far.

Many kids flourish. They find healing and love, and we watch in joy as God does miracle after miracle in their lives. Others, however, leave too soon. Some of them fall. But I trust that what we've sown will take root. That even in their darkest moments, they'll remember the place where they were safe, where someone believed in them, and where God's love was real. And maybe—just maybe—that will be enough to guide them home.

My husband wrote a book called *Dancing on the Water*, which is about the many miracles we have witnessed over the past forty years. This story isn't just about Peter's fear; it's about his courage to step out. It's not just about sinking; it's about the saving hand of Jesus. Peter may have doubted, but at least he walked. The others stayed in the boat. Only Peter knew what it felt like to stand on the water—even if just for a moment—and be rescued by the One who controls the storm.

For those of us who have dared to follow God into unknown waters, Peter's story rings true. We've walked by faith when there was no visible path. We've stepped out when staying put would've been safer. And yes, we've sunk more than once. But the hand of Jesus has never failed to lift us up. As my husband says, after walking on water for so long, now we're dancing on it.

But even after all these years, I still need to hear His voice whisper, "Come." That word—simple, powerful—is what keeps me going.

Every stage of life brings its own set of challenges. In my younger years, I battled fear of the unknown. Now, with more years behind me, I sometimes battle fear of the known: what I've seen, what I've walked through, what still lies ahead. Doubts try to creep in. Not doubts about who God is—I've seen too much of His goodness to question that—but doubts about circumstances, about provision, about the future. Real human doubts that settle deep into the heart.

I wish I could say I always live in hyper-faith, boldly stepping out without hesitation. But that wouldn't be honest.

The truth is, I can relate to Peter. A lot.

He gets a bad rap sometimes. People remember how he doubted, how he sank, how he denied Jesus three times. They talk about his impulsive words and reckless moments. But I see something different in Peter. I see someone who tried. Someone who got out of the boat. Someone who wanted to be close to Jesus, even if he didn't always get it right.

I see myself in him. I've had moments of boldness and moments of fear. I've spoken when I should have stayed quiet and remained silent when I should have spoken. I've stepped out in faith, only to sink into worry. And yet Jesus still reaches out His hand.

He doesn't withdraw. He doesn't roll His eyes or sigh in disappointment. He doesn't shame me. He just says again, "Come."

So I walk.

I walk toward Him, even when my steps are slow and shaky. I walk when the water looks impossible. I walk when I feel completely unqualified. I've learned something over the years: Faith doesn't grow by pretending to be fearless. It grows when I cling to Him in the middle of the storm, when I let Him steady my trembling hand.

Faith doesn't grow by pretending to be fearless. It grows when I cling to Him in the middle of the storm.

As long as my hand stays in His, I can keep walking. And sometimes—in the most unexpected moments—I find myself dancing.

God knows exactly who I am. He sees it all. And somehow my weakness doesn't scare Him off. It doesn't disappoint Him. The worst thing I could do is try to hide from Him, to pretend I've got it all together when I don't. To act like someone I'm not, when He already knows the real me—and loves me anyway.

I don't have to be superhuman. I don't have to be charismatic, or polished, or perfect. I just have to trust the One who is all-powerful.

He is strong where I am weak.

He is steady when I am unsure.

He is faithful, even when I falter.

And somehow, with all my flaws, He still chooses to use me.

The kids at Nana's House need to know that everyone struggles with something. No one has it all together—not me, not them, not anyone. Aiming to do our best and grow in character is a good goal, but being "perfect" isn't the ultimate target. What matters more is being humble, knowing that God loves us and that His love was never meant to be hoarded or used as a weapon. His love is meant to be shared.

We try to teach them that being a strong person doesn't mean being the loudest voice in the room or having all the answers. In fact, believing there's only one "right" way to live, parent, or even do church and worship can make our hearts small. The moment we open our eyes to the truth that life is full of nuance and diversity, our ability to love and accept others expands beautifully.

The truth is that weak people often struggle to handle differences. They can only love those who agree with them—who vote like them, think like them, parent like them, worship like them. But that's not love; that's control. And that's not the kind of community we're trying to build.

Life isn't about being the expert. It's about pointing people to the One who is. It's about letting God's love do its work in us and through us. I don't have all the answers, but I'm learning to keep my heart open—to listen, to stay soft, and to let love be the loudest thing about me.

Loving people is hard at times. It's far easier just to correct them, dismiss them, or throw our opinions like stones. But that's not what changes lives. Real love is patient. It leans in. It makes space for others to grow at their own pace. And that's what I hope these kids remember—not just how to behave, but how to love.

I count it one of the greatest privileges of my life to work with the children of Nana's House. I was born to do this. It's more than a calling. It's the very heartbeat of who I am. Every story, every child, every late-night cry and early-morning breakthrough—it's all amazing.

And it's not just about the children inside our home, either. We are dreaming beyond our walls. Currently, we're building a learning center in front of Nana's House where kids who have been told they'll never make it will rise, complete their education, earn their diplomas, and possibly even attend college. We want to offer opportunity where there was none and hope where there was once only despair.

Many lives have already been transformed because of Nana's House. And we aren't done. We want to keep going. We want to keep loving, rescuing, equipping, and sending out whole, healed people for many more years to come.

My own story started in tragedy. I was born into a storm of chaos after my grandparents' murder. God took all that wreckage and confusion and turned it into beauty. He always does that. Beauty rises from ashes. And now I live surrounded by what I can only call beautiful chaos—because even when life is messy, God's grace is constantly rebuilding, always redeeming.

Interestingly, as my parents aged, and as I grew older and wiser too, my eyes opened to things I had once misunderstood. I began to see them not just as the flawed people I had wrestled with growing up, but as complex, wounded souls trying to find their way through the pain they never fully named. They carried secrets. They carried shame. And that shame weighed them down like a heavy coat they couldn't take off. I wish they could have seen the beauty that surrounded them, the legacy of love that was theirs as well.

In the end, I saw them as eccentric, funny, heartbreaking, and tender. They both had Alzheimer's, and as the disease peeled back the layers of their guarded selves, they made me laugh and they made me cry. Their flaws didn't disappear—they just became part of the picture. And, strangely and beautifully, I was filled with love for them. I saw them through the eyes of grace. God loved them just as they were, and He died for them. I have their Bibles—two precious treasures—covered in their handwritten notes. They clung to Jesus, and that gives me peace.

Recently, we discovered that my dad had two children we didn't know about. A DNA test revealed two new siblings—a new family. And to be honest, getting to know them has been a gift. It's as if God keeps writing more chapters to this wild, messy, and beautiful story.

Life is never a straight line. It's twists and turns and heartbreak and laughter. It's disappointment and redemption. But through it all, I've learned this: When you place your chaos in God's hands, He doesn't throw it back at you. He shapes it. He mends it. And He makes something beautiful out of what seemed unfixable.

It's all beautiful chaos. And God rebuilds the brokenness with His grace.

About Heart4Mexico

Since 1998, our nonprofit organization Heart4Mexico has assisted in providing life-giving transformation to Mexican communities through practical, Christ-centered ministries. These include church planting, an orphanage for children, an accredited School of Missions, and short-term missions teams. Heart4Mexico serves as a fountain of renewed hope and second chances to those we seek to serve, and we strive to maintain trustworthy standards and provide life-changing outcomes that will impact these communities for generations to come.

If you would like to support national pastors, missionaries, and projects, you can find more information or make financial contributions at h4mx.org.

Email: info@h4mx.org
Phone (US): 818-388-4835

In addition to Beautiful Chaos, Heart4Mexico has published other books that share real stories from the mission field and invite readers into a deeper walk with Christ. These books reflect the heart of Heart4Mexico — raw faith, real people, and God's redemptive power at work in broken places.

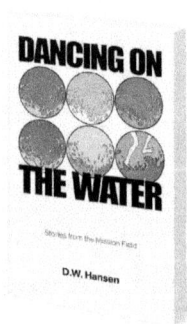

Dancing on the Water
by Dwight Hansen

A collection of powerful, honest stories from decades of missionary life, centered on learning to trust God in impossible situations and step out in faith.

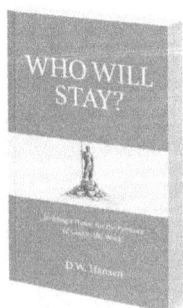

Who Will Stay
by Heart4Mexico

A compelling look at the cost of calling and the question every missionary must face: who will remain faithful when the work becomes difficult? This book challenges readers to perseverance, faithfulness, and long-term commitment to God's work.